the inne

7

the inner winner

Performance Psychology Tactics
That Give You An Unfair Advantage

simon hazeldine

⬤ bookshaker

First Published in Great Britain 2006
by New Breed Publishing

This Edition Published in Great Britain 2012
by www.BookShaker.com

To Mum and Dad with all my love.
To my wife Karen with all my love.
I admire and love you for (amongst many things)
your bravery and positive mental attitude.
To my son Thomas with all my love.
You remind me how a winner thinks
and behaves every single day.

Acknowledgements

To Jamie O'Keefe for publishing the first edition of *The Inner Winner*. To the team at Bookshaker: Joe for all his input, encouragement and design work; Lucy for her eagle-eyed editing skills.

Contents

Introduction

Congratulations on taking the decision to join a very special group of people. You have chosen to join the ever growing group of people who understand that in order to be the very best that they can be, they *must* utilise the immense power of the human mind.

The Inner Winner contains proven performance psychology tactics that you can use to enhance your performance in sport, business and life in general. This book takes powerful psychological performance strategies and makes them easy to understand and use. There is no psychological 'mumbo jumbo', just hard hitting performance tactics that work.

All of the tactics contained within *The Inner Winner* are based upon proven scientific research. These powerful and proven psychological tactics can be easily learned and applied.

No matter what level of performance you are currently operating at, these psychological tactics can enhance it further. You can, and will, get a boost from the most powerful performance enhancer of all – *your mind*.

Today, almost without exception, professional sportspeople and elite athletes train physically *and* psychologically. More and more sports people are turning to mental training to get a competitive edge and to ensure that they realise their full potential. However, the advantages that performance psychology tactics deliver are most certainly not confined to the world of sport.

The very same psychological strategies that elite sportspeople use can easily be applied to business, sales, education and numerous other areas of your life.

The Inner Winner combines a comprehensive collection of established and proven psychological performance strategies with one of the most powerful fields of modern psychology, Neuro Linguistic Programming or, as it is more commonly known, NLP.

NLP has been described as 'the psychology of human excellence'.

NLP provides:

1. Methods to discover the patterns of thinking and behaviour that produce excellence in any field. NLP enables the structure of these patterns of excellence to be identified and made available to other people. NLP allows us to work out exactly how someone who is excellent at some activity or skill produces this excellence and makes it possible to transfer this ability to other people.

2. Highly effective ways of thinking and communication that are used by outstanding people to produce outstanding results.

The phrase 'Neuro Linguistic Programming' covers three very simple areas:

Neuro

This acknowledges the fundamental idea that all behaviour stems from our neurological processes of sight, hearing, smell, taste, touch and feeling. We experience our world through our five senses; we make 'sense' of the information and then act upon it. Our neurology covers not only our invisible thought processes, but also our visible physiological reactions to ideas and events. One simply reflects the other at the physical level. Your body and mind are not separate, but are an integrated system.

Linguistic

This acknowledges that we use language to order our thoughts and behaviour and to communicate with others. The language that we use, both with others and with ourselves has a powerful influence over our behaviour and therefore the results we achieve.

Programming

This refers to ways that we can choose to organise our ideas and actions to produce results. NLP provides us with an ability to organise our communication and neurological systems so that we can achieve specific results. We all have programmes or strategies that we operate on an ongoing basis, and NLP offers the opportunity (perhaps for the first time) to have a conscious awareness of what has previously been unconscious processing.

No matter what area of your life you wish to apply these performance psychology strategies to, *The Inner Winner* will assist you in achieving your full potential.

The field of psychology can seem daunting as it is often based upon complex theories. *The Inner Winner* will explain these concepts in simple language. You will not need a degree in psychology to understand them.

Although the psychological theories upon which they are based may appear complex, all of the hard work has been done for you. *The Inner Winner* will make powerful psychological methods of performance enhancement easy to understand and use.

You will not only learn what to do, you will also learn why and how the various techniques and concepts work. This will be done in a very straightforward manner.

In this way your knowledge and skills will be built. I believe that it is very important that you understand the theories that lie behind the various critical performance psychology strategies and how to apply them in a practical manner.

By the time you have finished *The Inner Winner*, you will have a god understanding of the power of the human mind and a brand new and powerful set of skills to transform your performance.

I wish you every success in your quest for excellence.

Simon Hazeldine MSc FInstSMM

What Are Performance Psychology Tactics?

Scientifically proven to enhance performance

This book contains a powerful series of psychological tactics that have been scientifically proven to enhance performance.

As mentioned earlier, the benefits of performance psychology are not limited to the world of sport. Yes, you may wish to become a champion athlete. You can also become a champion in business achievement, a champion in educational achievement, a champion salesperson or a champion parent. Champions are people who excel. Champions focus their energy upon becoming exceptional. Don't sell yourself short – be a champion.

What does it take to be a champion?

The answer is relatively simple to describe but not so easy to achieve. It takes a lot of practice and a lot of hard work. However, there are many practical things you can do to build upon the efforts that you make.

One way of thinking about what it takes to be a success is a concept called 'The Winner's Triangle'.

The winner's triangle has three component elements: Attitude, Skills and Knowledge.

I often ask participants at my seminars to consider what makes a winner. I ask them to consider how much Attitude, Skills and Knowledge each contribute to making someone a winner. I then ask them how much, out of 100%, they would attribute to the element of attitude. The answer from my audience is nearly always the same – they believe that attitude accounts for 80% or more of winning.

Whilst I agree that attitude (or 'the will to win' as it is sometimes described) is obviously important, attitude alone is just not enough.

In order to be a winner you need good knowledge of your chosen area and the skills required to succeed in it. I believe the percentages are more likely to be:

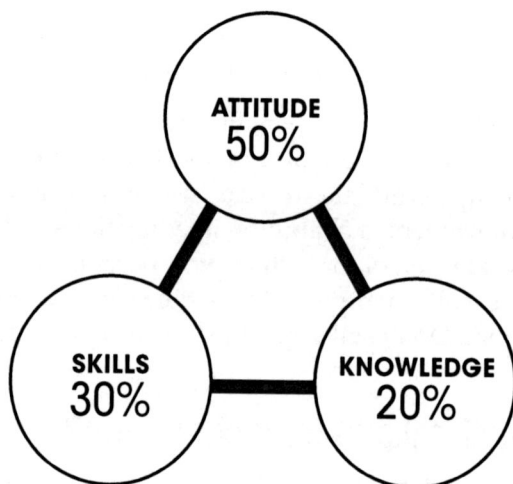

Attitude is, of course, vitally important. However, I stress that on its own it is just not enough. As I joke with my seminar participants:

> Question: What do you get if you motivate an idiot?

> Answer: A motivated idiot!

In keeping with this concept, *The Inner Winner* will give you the knowledge about how and why the various performance psychology tactics work. You will also be shown how to develop the skills to apply this knowledge so that you can enhance your current performance. These elements will help you to further develop your winning attitude.

The Inner Winner is not a trite, positive thinking book. We will be going much deeper than a shallow 'rah rah' approach to motivation and performance.

Please do not misunderstand me; I am a great believer in 'positive thinking'. Adopting a positive mindset brings huge benefits. What I do not subscribe to is some of the rubbish that is spouted about positive attitude.

Some speakers and writers will have you believe that if you have a positive attitude everything in life will be wonderful. This is naïve and stupid. Life will invariably have its challenges and having a positive attitude will help you to deal with these challenges far better than a negative attitude. However, in order to thrive, much more than a 'looking at the world through rose coloured glasses' approach is needed.

An analogy that I once heard, likened this naïve positive attitude as being similar to walking into your garden, seeing the weeds infesting the flower beds and pretending they weren't there. You can imagine the 'positive thinker' avoiding looking at the weeds and chanting: 'There are no weeds, there are no weeds!'

If you adopt this naïve attitude the weeds will take eventually overtake your garden. A practical and realistic positive attitude would acknowledge the presence of the weeds and then do something about them, such as digging them up.

I am sure you appreciate the difference. Having a positive mental attitude is important and recommended. This does not mean you do not acknowledge the challenges and problems that may occur. On the contrary, if they do occur you do something about them and get them sorted out. This is a *practical* and *positive* attitude.

With this concept in mind *The Inner Winner* will teach you a comprehensive and practical approach to performance psychology. *The Inner Winner* is not, and will never be, about naïve optimism or impractical positive thinking.

You will be shown proven and practical ways to build and develop, for example, your mental toughness and focus. You will discover the difference that makes the difference.

You will learn practical ways to develop a well-founded, positive and winning bank of knowledge, skills and attitude.

Why you must use Performance Psychology

As mentioned previously, in recent years an increasing number of sportspeople have begun to realise that, in order to achieve their full potential, it is no longer enough to just train physically.

I repeat: no matter how hard or how long you train, physical training on its own is no longer sufficient. Ever increasing numbers of athletes are turning to psychological training to give them an advantage.

And the world of business is catching on fast. My business consultancy, E3, specialises in enhancing organisational performance. Part of the unique E3 approach is to always underpin, for example, our sales training with performance psychology tactics and strategies. Wise companies the world over are starting to look at the field of performance psychology to gain a competitive advantage. And wise individuals are exploring performance psychology so that they use it to benefit in countless areas of their life.

The roots of performance psychology lie in history. Early Greek and Asian cultures acknowledged and emphasised the interdependence of body and mind. It was seen as central to not only improving performance, but playing a vital role in personal development in a broader sense.

As early as the 1920s, books were being published on the subject of sports psychology, and some of the first sports psychology laboratories were being established.

However, it was not until the 1960s that the area began to increase its prominence. During the height of Communism, Soviet and Eastern bloc athletes were observed to be winning a disproportionate number of medals in international and Olympic events.

The suspicion was that this was due to performance-enhancing drugs. What began to emerge was evidence that the psychological training of Soviet and Eastern bloc athletes far exceeded that of their Western counterparts.

From the 1960s and through the 70s, 80s and 90s, the area of psychological training and sports psychology developed and flourished. Now in the 21st century, very few, if any, professional athletes do not have psychological aspects built into their training programme.

As discussed earlier, performance psychology can be used to gain a competitive advantage over other athletes in competitions and tournaments.

It can also be used to powerfully support physical training. By training the body and the mind, significant performance advancements can be achieved.

Outside the world of sport you can combine performance psychology with almost any other field of endeavour and get an enhanced result. For example, if you need to take an important exam you need to study. However, if you add some elements of performance psychology, like creating high levels of motivation to do the hours of required study, keeping in a calm state and maintaining a deep level of concentration throughout the exam, you will produce a better result. Once you have experienced the benefits of performance psychology you will find yourself utilising it in many ways, many times a day.

Performance psychology can also be used to improve your understanding and development of yourself. This can enable you to realise more of your individual potential.

Performance psychology will undoubtedly have significant benefits in other areas of your personal life too.

By the time you have read *The Inner Winner* and applied what you have learned:

- You will be a lot clearer and focused on what you want to achieve in your life.
- You will understand the factors that motivate you to succeed.
- Your confidence in yourself and your abilities will have been enhanced.
- You will know how to alter your beliefs about yourself and your abilities.
- You will have more commitment and self-discipline.

- You will know how to put yourself into any state of mind you desire – within seconds.
- Your concentration will have improved dramatically.
- You will know how to cope with stress and tension.
- You will be able to relax easily and quickly.
- You will be able to use self-hypnosis to programme your mind for success.

As mentioned earlier, this book goes far beyond what is commonly known as 'positive thinking'. You will be shown how to develop a complete portfolio of performance psychology strategies that will support you in many areas of your life.

There are a number of core elements that make up performance psychology. This book will enable you to identify and understand the specific psychological factors that can enable you to tap into more of your unique potential as a human being.

This collection of psychological strategies can empower you to enhance your personal performance.

By combining these it is possible for you to achieve the ideal and sometimes elusive 'peak performance' state.

What is Peak Performance?

Peak performance has been described as 'behaviour that exceeds one's average performance' or 'an episode of superior functioning'.

Peak performance is about going beyond what you think is currently possible. It may not necessarily be about being better than other people. It is about being the very best that you can be.

In the sporting world, an experience of peak performance will often result in a 'personal best' performance from an athlete. These experiences are the ultimate high, the thrilling moment that athletes work for in their pursuit of excellence.

According to research, peak performance is more likely to occur when an individual's skill level matches the demand or challenge of the situation. This is interesting as it suggests that peak performance can be attained at whatever level an individual is working at.

A study of athletes' 'greatest moments' in sport reported that over 80% of the athletes surveyed had the following perceptions:

- A loss of fear – there was no fear of failure.
- They were not thinking about their performance.
- They were totally immersed in what they were doing.
- They had a narrow focus of attention.
- Their performance was effortless.
- They felt in complete control.
- There was some time and/or space distortion with time usually seeming to slow down.
- The universe appeared to be integrated and unified.[1]

Other athletes have described it as 'being possessed yet in total control'. They described participating in their sport with 'profound intensity, total concentration and an enthusiasm that bordered on joy'.

The following quotation summarises the unique peak performance state:

> 'I felt like I could do almost anything, as if I were in complete control. I really felt confident and positive. I felt physically very relaxed, but really energized and pumped up. I experienced virtually no anxiety or fear, and the whole experience was enjoyable. I experienced a very real sense of calmness and quiet inside, and everything just seemed to flow automatically. Even though I was hustling, it was all very effortless.'[2]

The psychological tactics that you will learn in *The Inner Winner* will assist you in achieving this peak performance state – it can be experienced in many areas of life.

In order to do this, there are several core elements of performance psychology that we will be looking at in considerable detail.

---

1   Ravizza, K. (1977) Peak experience in sport. *Journal of Humanistic Psychology*
2   Loehr, J.E. (1984) How to overome stress and play at your peak all the time. *Tennis*

These elements have been specifically selected as they have been identified by psychological research as being the traits that mean the difference between winners and losers.[3][4][5][6]

Whilst most areas if life are not so clearly divided into 'winners' and 'losers', most people when asked would prefer to think of themselves as a winner. In addition, the performance psychology strategies employed by winning athletes provide a rich vein of evidence to be explored.

If we study winners and work out what they do, we can then replicate what they do by copying their strategies.

The core elements of Performance Psychology

The research conducted into the psychological difference between winning and losing athletes describes some very specific areas.

These areas are the core elements of performance psychology that we need to focus upon.

The core areas are:

1. Goal-setting
2. Motivation
3. State Management
4. Concentration and Mental Focus
5. Confidence
6. Coping Strategies

3   Mahoney, M.J., & Avener, M. (1977) Psychology of the elite athlete: An exploratory study. *Cognitive Therapy and Research*
4   Highlen, P.S. et al (1979) Psychological characteristics of successful and nonsuccessful elite wrestlers: An exploratory study. *Journal of Sport Psychology*
5   Gould, D., et al (1981) Psychological characteristics of successful and nonsuccessful Big Ten wrestlers. *Journal of Sport Psychology*
6   Mahoney, M.J., et al (1987) Psychological skills and exceptional athletic performance, *The Sport Psychologist*

Goal Setting	Motivation	State Management

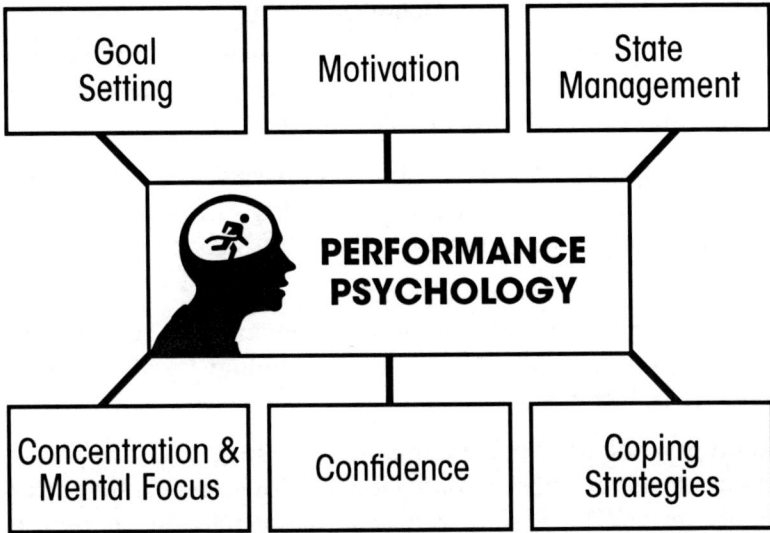

PERFORMANCE PSYCHOLOGY

Concentration & Mental Focus	Confidence	Coping Strategies

You will be introduced to these areas in this chapter, and each of these areas will be covered in detail in subsequent chapters.

Goal-setting

Numerous psychological studies have proved that properly set goals improve performance. A comprehensive review of over 100 psychological studies on goal-setting concluded that 'the beneficial effect of goal-setting on task performance is one of the most robust and replicable findings in the psychological literature'. In other words goal-setting works.[7]

Goals set specific targets that motivate people to take action by focusing attention, increasing effort and intensity and encouraging persistence in the face of failure.

A goal is something you want to accomplish. It is the object or aim of an action. Goals can also be set to achieve a specific standard of proficiency on a task, usually within a specified time limit.

Having specific goals will lead you to higher levels of performance than having no goals or 'easy' goals or 'do your best' goals.

7   Locke, E.A., and Latham, G.P. (1990) *A Theory of Goal Setting and Task Performance*, Prentice-Hall

Motivation

To say that elite athletes are highly motivated individuals is a statement of the obvious. However, the subject of motivation is more complex than many people realise.

Maintaining motivation over the long period that is necessary for mastery in any field is an area worthy of further study, as is maintaining motivation in the face of setback, failure and defeat.

A variety of factors influence motivation and these can be both external (known as 'extrinsic' by psychologists) and internal (known as 'intrinsic').

Some psychologists believe that motivation to improve performance develops out of dissatisfaction with your current performance levels. There is no doubt that dissatisfaction (sometimes referred to as 'inspirational dissatisfaction') can be a powerful motivator.

However, it is thought that a more effective motivation is evidence of your success, also described as positive reinforcement. If you become aware of your progress and how your training is paying off, your motivation should increase.

State Management

In order to perform certain tasks successfully, we need to be in the right 'state of mind'. In case this important concept of 'state' is new to you, here is a brief explanation.

When people are emotionally or physically at a low ebb we say they are in 'a bit of a state'.

State can be defined as the combination of all of the thoughts, emotions and physiology that we are experiencing and expressing at any one moment.

Elite athletes will be trained by sports psychologists to get themselves into an appropriate state of activation (readiness to perform) for the specific events in which they are participating.

It is an over-simplification to think of activation as 'psyching up' or 'psyching down'. To achieve peak performance, an appropriate level of activation (known as 'optimum activation') is required for the specific task at hand.

There are a number of specific strategies and techniques that can be employed to achieve optimum activation states and we will discuss them in greater depth in a later chapter.

Concentration and Mental Focus

Loss of concentration can impair performance and maintaining concentration can be a problem for some individuals. It is very rare to find people who are not interested in increasing their powers of concentration and focus.

Concentration is about focusing the mind upon one thing, often to the exclusion of others. More importantly, the focus of attention is crucial in determining whether the concentration is appropriate or not.

Allowing all your attention to be focused on a recent failure in performance is unlikely to help your performance improve. You get more of what you focus on.

Coping Strategies

Let's not pull any punches – if you want to be a champion in any field then you need to learn to cope with adversity. Attaining any significant and challenging goal will invariably expose you to hurdles, obstacles, setbacks and stress. Indeed, by committing yourself to any form of significant achievement in any field of endeavour, you are choosing to expose yourself to adversity and stress.

Stress is the body's reaction to a change that requires a physical, mental or emotional adjustment or response. In its simplest form, *coping* is the way individuals deal with these types of demands.

Elite performers generally seem able to control their anxiety and generate an appropriate state that enables them to perform at their very best most of the time.

We will explore this area in detail and empower you with effective ways to cope with and thrive upon the demands of achieving exceptional levels of performance.

Confidence

One definition of confidence is having belief and optimism in your own ability to perform well. Elite performers have higher levels of self-confidence.[8]

Further research has indicated that in stressful situations, individuals low in self-confidence tend to experience greater anxiety and give up more readily.[9]

It is therefore vitally important to commit to improving in this area. Performance psychology can deliver very rapid improvements in self-confidence.

By the time you have finished reading *The Inner Winner*, you will possess a good understanding of these six performance psychology factors – and much more besides.

It has been said that, 'knowledge is power'. I disagree. It isn't that knowledge isn't important. It is important. It is one of the three component elements of 'The Winner's Triangle'. However, knowledge is only power when it is applied. If you want to benefit from the power of psychological training then you need to practise the techniques, tactics and strategies of performance psychology.

You cannot learn anything by reading a book – you have to practise. In the same way, you cannot learn how to harness the power of performance psychology simply by reading this book – you need to put what you learn into practice.

So please don't just read this book, use it as a training guide and put what you learn into practice. Then you will be able to fully utilise the most powerful performance device in the known universe – your mind.

8   Mahoney , M.J. (1987) Psychological skills and exceptional athletic performance, *The Sports Psychologist*
9   Bandura, A (1982) Self –efficacy mechanism in human agency, *American Psychologist*

Champion or Runner Up?

The psychological differences between winners and losers

What exactly does it take to be a winner rather than a loser? What are the vital differences that separate the champions from those who just never seem to make it?

In the world of sport it obviously takes countless hours of physical training and hard work. In theory it is always possible for someone with sufficient dedication to train as physically hard as the champions.

In the world of business it also takes hard work, commitment and dedication. However, it is always possible for a competing business to work as hard, with as much commitment and dedication. It doesn't take very long for any business to copy the products, services and business practices of one of their competitors.

At the top levels in sport and business it is often psychological factors that separate the winners from the losers and the elite from the non-elite. Someone may try to copy exactly what you do in order to get the same results as you. What they cannot copy is what goes on inside your mind.

People who know and understand how to use performance psychology tactics can gain an edge over their competitors.

So what are the psychological factors that make up this 'winner's edge'?

A number of studies have been conducted to determine the difference between successful and unsuccessful athletes.[10] [11] [12] [13] [14] [15] [16] [17] [18] [19]

Their conclusions are worth exploring to see how we can use performance psychology tactics to enhance our performance in sport, business and life.

The following is a summary of these studies undertaken by sports psychologists to determine the psychological differences between successful and unsuccessful athletes.

Winning athletes had higher levels of self-confidence

A psychological study of over 700 athletes from 23 sports concluded that elite performers had higher and more stable levels of self-confidence than non-elite athletes.[20]

The winning athletes believed in themselves more than the less successful athletes

Linked to the area of self-confidence is self-belief. Recent psychological research with elite international athletes into 'mental toughness' concluded that having an unshakeable belief in your ability to achieve your competition goals was the most important attribute of the mentally tough performer.[21]

10   Mahoney , M.J. (1987) Psychological skills and exceptional athletic performance, *The Sports Psychologist*
11   Mahoney, M.J., and Avener, M. (1977) Psychology of the elite athlete: An exploratory study, *Cognitive Therapy and Research*
12   Jones, G., et al Intensity and interpretation of anxiety symptoms in elite and non-elite sports performers, *Personal Individual Differences*
13   Jones, G., et al Predisposition to experience debilitative and facilitative anxiety in elite and non-elite performers, *The Sports Psychologist*
14   Orlick, T., and Partington, J. (1987) The sport psychology consultant: Analysis of critical components as viewed by Canadian Olympic athletes, *The Sport Psychologist*
15   Kingston, K.M., and Hardy, L. (1994) When are some goals more beneficial than others?, *Journal of Sport Sciences*
16   Jones, J.G. and Hardy, L. (1990) Stress in sport: Experiences of some elite performers. In G. Jones and L. Hardy (eds), *Stress and Performance in Sport*
17   Orlick, T. and Partington, J. (1988) Mental links to excellence, *The Sport Psychologist*
18   Highlen, P.S. et al (1979) Psychological characteristics of successful and nonsuccessful elite wrestlers: An exploratory study. *Journal of Sport Psychology*
19   Gould, D., et al (1981) Psychological characteristics of successful and nonsuccessful Big Ten wrestlers. *Journal of Sport Psychology*
20   Mahoney , M.J. (1987) Psychological skills and exceptional athletic performance, *The Sports Psychologist*
21   Jones, G. (2002) What is this thing called mental toughness? An investigation of elite sports performers. *Journal of Applied Sports Psychology*

Winning athletes had better levels of concentration and were less likely to be distracted than less successful athletes

The ability to concentrate, to focus the mind upon one thing, often to the exclusion of all others, contributes significantly to enhanced performance. In the world of sport the athlete who becomes easily distracted will find their performance impaired.

Winning athletes made more use of mental rehearsal and positive mental imagery than less successful athletes

Almost 100% of Olympic athletes surveyed by sports psychologists reported using mental rehearsal.[22] Elite athletes use this technique for one reason and one reason only – it works. Mental rehearsal is a very powerful performance enhancement method.

Psychological research demonstrates that mental rehearsal combined with physical practise is a more effective method of performance enhancement than physical practise alone.

Winning athletes used more positive self-talk than less successful athletes

A survey of winning and losing gymnasts concluded that one of the differentiating factors was that the winning gymnasts made far more use of positive self-talk than the losing athletes.[23] As simple as it may sound, talking positively to yourself is a powerful method of performance enhancement.

Winning athletes were less anxious before and during competition than less successful athletes

Surveys of winning athletes demonstrate that not only do they accept that competition anxiety is inevitable, they believe that they can cope with it. In addition there is evidence that many elite athletes thrive on the pressure of competition and believe it brings out the best in them.[24]

22   Orlick, T. and Partington, I., (1987) The sport psychology consultant: Analysis of critical components as viewed by Olympic athletes, *The Sport Psychologist*
23   Mahoney, M.J. and Avener, M., (1977) Psychology of the elite athlete: An exploratory study, *Cognitive Therapy and Research*
24   Jones, G. (1994) Intensity and interpretation of anxiety symptoms in elite and non-elite sports performers, *Personal Individual Differences*

Winning athletes controlled their anxiety
better than less successful athletes

Winners are able to employ a variety of techniques to manage their state and how they are feeling. These abilities make it possible for them to control their anxiety and prevent it from interfering with their performance.

Winning athletes had a higher ability to rebound
from mistakes than less successful athletes

Surveys of elite athletes report that they do not believe that anyone's rise to the top is completely smooth, and that there will always be setbacks along the way. Indeed they also reported that they use these setbacks as a way of increasing their determination to succeed![25]

By modelling the beliefs and performance psychology tactics of elite athletes, it is possible for anyone to enhance their performance, to develop their winner's edge and achieve champion status – in whatever field of endeavour they choose.

---

25   Jones, G. (2002) What is this thing called mental toughness? An investigation of elite sports performers. *Journal of Applied Sports Psychology*

Get Sorted

> 'If you don't know where you are going –
> any road will take you there.'
> **LEWIS CARROLL**

The importance of knowing where you are going

This is one of the most important sections in *The Inner Winner*. Why is it so important? Because it will guide you to understanding what it is that you want from your life.

Why is it so important to know what you want? When I am working with people from the sporting or business world, I always start with getting them to answer one of the most important questions:

'What do you want?'

This might, on first reading, seem to be a simple, four word question. But I rarely find anyone who can answer this question properly. After you have completed the exercises in this chapter, you will be able to.

Imagine for a moment that you are setting out on a journey in a car to get to a specific place. First and foremost you would need to know where you are going. You would need to know where it was and how you would know when you had arrived at your destination. You would also plan your route to get to where you want to go. You would not drive around aimlessly hoping for the best, would you? This seems obvious, doesn't it?

As obvious as this example may be, though, in my experience most people do not have a clear destination or a plan of how to get there – even for the most important areas of their life.

Sir Edmund Hilary and Sherpa Tensing did not climb to the top of Mount Everest by wandering around and hoping for the best. They had a very specific goal (and a specific plan of how to accomplish this.

Why should it be any different for you?

The American motivational speaker Zig Ziglar challenges his audiences by asking them: *'Are you a wandering generality or are you a meaningful specific?'*

Do you lack clear direction and purpose, or do have clear goals that focus your attention and action?

I ask participants at my performance psychology seminars two questions:

'Please put your hand up if you have made a will or if you have some form of life insurance.'

The majority of people in the room usually put their hand up in response to this question. I then ask:

'Please put your hand up if you have a clearly defined set of goals for all of the key areas of your life and you have them written down.'

I am lucky if more than a few people put their hand up in a room of 100+ people. I then make the somewhat tongue-in-cheek observation that the people in the room have put more effort into preparing for death than they have for living their life.

Do you have clear goals upon which you focus and take action, or do you, in common with the majority of people, have very little idea of what you want to achieve and lead a somewhat aimless life?

I appreciate that this may sound harsh, but this is an important area, and I want you to understand the vital importance and power of setting specific goals.

A number of studies have identified that setting goals is one of

the key attributes of high performing people.[26]

---

26   Locke, E.A., and Latham, G.P. (1990) *A Theory of Goal Setting and Task Performance*, Prentice-Hall

Why set goals?

You need to set yourself goals because they consistently improve performance. Goal-setting is a powerful technique for enhancing your performance and achievements.

The psychological research on goal-setting is impressive. A clear pattern of results has emerged. A comprehensive review of over 100 psychological studies on goal-setting concluded that, 'the beneficial effect of goal-setting on task performance is one of the most robust and replicable findings in the psychological literature'.[27]

Goal-setting is a powerful technique that clearly and consistently facilitates performance.

Goal-setting influences performance in a number of important ways:

- Goals focus attention and action on important aspects of performance.
- Goals set specific standards that motivate individuals to take direct action.
- Goals increase not only immediate effort and intensity, but also help to prolong effort and increase persistence.
- Goals also prompt the development of new problem-solving and learning strategies.

When setting goals, it is important to consider research that suggests to have difficult or challenging goals is far more effective in enhancing performance than 'easy' goals or general 'do your best' goals.

What are goals?

A goal is something that you want to accomplish. It is the object or aim of an action. The famous football coach, Sven Goran Erikkson said:

'Goals are the things we want to achieve. It is important to set them.'

---

27   Locke, E.A., and Latham, G.P. (1990) *A Theory of Goal Setting and Task Performance*, Prentice-Hall

Goals can also be set to achieve a specific standard of proficiency in a task, usually within a specified time limit.

It is very important to consider the different types of goals that you can set, as these can have significant impacts upon your performance and achievements.

There are three main categories of goals:

- Outcome Goals
- Performance Goals
- Process Goals

Outcome Goals focus on achieving specific results or outcomes. In sport these could include winning a gold medal, and in the business world achieving a number one market share position.

Performance Goals focus on improvements relative to your own past performance. For example, in the world of sport this could relate to an increase in the number of kilograms you can lift on a bench press, and in the business world to an increase in the number of sales calls made in a day. Performance goals can cover any *specific* and *measured* improvement.

Process Goals focus on the procedures which you will engage in during performance. For a martial artist this could be about maintaining a calm mental focus during competition, or in the world of business maintaining the same calm mental focus during important contract negotiations.

These three goal distinctions are important because evidence suggests that, depending upon circumstance, certain types of goals are more useful in changing behaviour (and therefore facilitating desired achievements) than other types of goals.

When people focus solely on outcome goals (or 'winning goals' as they are sometimes referred to), unrealistic future expectations can sometimes result. These expectations can lead to lower levels of confidence, decreased effort and a worsening of performance.

There is value in having a very clear outcome goal. Having a clear and solid idea of what you want to achieve can be very motivational and inspiring. However, outcome goals can be outside your control. To win the national championship you will need to beat many other competitors. They will also be aiming to win the national championships. Your outcome goal is not entirely under your control.

Therefore, to support your outcome goal it is vitally important that you have well-constructed performance and process goals. Performance and process goals are both under your control and are flexible. You cannot fully control how another competitor will behave but you do have total control over:

- The preparation and effort you put into improving your performance.
- The processes you focus on during performance.

What is known as 'Goal Proximity' is a further defining factor. You can set long-term and medium/short-term goals within the three categories of outcome, performance and process goals defined above.

Research suggests that having a combination of long and medium/short term goals produces the greatest performance improvements.[28]

The attainment of a series of short/medium term goals is particularly effective as they provide indicators of 'mastery' which can lead to enhanced confidence.

As you achieve each level of performance, this is motivational as it gives a sense of progress, a sense of achievement and provides the motivation to achieve the next performance goal.

What evidence is there about the power of setting goals?

Goal-setting as a motivational approach to enhancing performance is one of the most thoroughly researched areas of psychology. The psychological research on goal-setting is impressive in that it has been conducted in a variety of laboratory and field settings, and has used a wide variety of tasks and diverse samples of people including children, managers and unskilled workers.

28   Locke, E.A., and Latham, G.P. (1985) The application of goal setting to sport, *Journal of Sport Psychology*

I think it is important to re-emphasise the importance of goal setting by quoting a comprehensive review of well over 100 studies on goal-setting concluded: *'the beneficial effect of goal-setting on task performance is one of the most robust and replicable findings in the psychological literature'*.[29]

The theoretical explanations for the relationship between goal-setting and performance include:

1. Goals direct and focus your attention to important aspects of a specific task.
2. Goals help you to mobilise effort, for example setting a series of steps towards a goal will make you exhibit greater effort towards achieving your goal.
3. Goals not only increase immediate effort, but prolong effort and increase persistence.
4. Research has shown that you will often develop and employ new learning strategies through the process of setting and achieving goals.

How do I set goals?

When setting goals you need to consider three key factors:

Why you want to achieve your goal.

What are the personal benefits in achieving your goal? This provides the fuel to reach the goal.

What your goal is.

This provides direction.

How you are going to achieve your goal?

It can also be useful to consider *What if* you achieve your goal? This allows you to consider the future implications and possibilities of achieving your goal.

---

29   Locke, E.A., and Latham, G.P. (1990) *A Theory of Goal Setting and Task Performance*, Prentice-Hall

The Power of Why?

> 'I am the master of my fate; I am the captain of my soul.'
> **WILLIAM ERNEST HENLEY**

A goal answers the important question: 'What do you want?' However, prior to setting the goal it is important to answer the additional question: 'What do you really want?' This is accomplished by ensuring you are clear about which of your personal values and needs achieving your goal will support or satisfy.

> 'He who knows himself can see clearly.'
> **LAO TZU**

Your needs

We all have needs. Needs are the resources, people, feelings or environment that you must have in order to be your best.

Until your needs are satisfied, they may divert attention and energy that can be better invested elsewhere. For example, when we are hungry or thirsty we have a need for food or water. These very basic survival needs will tend to occupy us and most of our attention will be focused on satisfying them.

Whilst basic needs such as food and water may seem obvious, we all have a number of additional needs. By considering needs and including them in your goal-setting, it is possible to get some or all of your needs met on an ongoing basis.

This can increase not only your motivation to work at and achieve your goals, but also make the process of achieving them satisfying.

One useful model of human needs groups them into three broad categories:

1. Survival Needs
2. Emotional Needs
3. Fulfilment Needs

The three **Survival Needs** are:
- Food
- Water
- Shelter

These are very basic human needs. We all need food, water and shelter to survive. The survival instinct is one of the most basic and fundamental human (and other animal) characteristics.

Although it is rare to die of hunger and thirst in our welfare state society, these needs can still drive and affect our behaviour. These basic survival needs can be threatened with the prospect of someone losing their job and potential financial hardship.

Generally speaking, once we have satisfied the basic human survival needs we will then seek to satisfy our emotional needs.

The four **Emotional Needs** are:
- Control
- Variety
- Significance
- Connection

We all need some certainty in our lives. To varying degrees we need some sense of routine and comfort. We need some degree of control over various aspects of our lives – our working life, our home life, our hobbies, our relationships and so forth to feel comfortable. Imagine a life where nothing at all was certain! Generally the more control people feel they have the less stressed and anxious they feel.

If some aspects of our life become uncertain we can feel uncomfortable. For example, if you get a new boss who makes it very clear that 'there are going to be some major changes around here', then you may feel uncomfortable until you have some certainty about what is going to be happening.

A need that almost seems as if it is the very opposite of certainty is the need for variety. If absolutely everything was totally certain and nothing ever changed then life would not seem very interesting. Different people will need different amounts of variety. Some people will go on holiday to the same place year after year and this suits them. Other people will never go to the same place twice. They love variety.

The important thing is that you get the balance of certainty and variety that is right for you. Without any variety life could get stale; with too much it might become stressful and uncomfortable.

The very existence of cars such as BMW, Mercedes or Ferrari, designer clothing, Rolex and Gucci watches clearly demonstrate the human need for significance. To varying degrees people have a need to be significant.

In some people this manifests itself in the purchase of status symbols (cars, houses, expensive holidays, jewellery etc); in others it is in the attainment of specific levels of achievement (becoming the director of a company, achieving a black belt in the martial arts, winning a gold medal, having a book published); and yet others in more personal ways, such as becoming a parent.

The final emotional need is connection. Most human beings like being around other human beings. Most of us also enjoy being in loving relationships with other human beings. This shows itself in our need for friendships, social relationships and family relationships. Meeting the need for connection can also facilitate us being able to satisfy other human desires such as reproduction of the species.

As with the survival needs, once we have satisfied our emotional needs we will seek to have our fulfilment needs satisfied.

The two **Fulfilment Needs** are:
- Growth
- Contribution Beyond Self

Many people will seek some form of growth in their life. They will want to feel satisfied that they are growing as a person and that they are making progress.

This need will manifest itself in self-improvement activities, educational programmes, spiritual development and so forth.

Many people, as evidenced by philanthropic acts like working for charity or putting effort into community activities, have a need to contribute beyond self. Many of us like to 'do our bit' to 'put something back'. This can be very satisfying.

So, we have explored some possible needs that you may have. In summary these are:

Survival Needs
- Food
- Water
- Shelter

Emotional Needs
- Control
- Variety
- Significance
- Connection

Fulfilment Needs
- Growth
- Contribution Beyond Self

The theory is that human behaviour is strongly influenced by our desire to satisfy these needs. Until our needs are met we want to get them satisfied and this desire is a powerful motivator. By becoming aware of your own individual and personal needs, you can incorporate these into the goals that you set for yourself.

In this way, you will be motivated to achieve your goals. You will also gain satisfaction from not only the achievement of your goals but from the efforts you have to put into getting them.

Below is a list of possible needs. Take some time to consider the needs that you feel are most important to you. You may wish to consider needs that are not on the list. The list is not exhaustive, they are just suggestions. Please feel free to add any other examples of needs that may occur to you.

Which of these needs are important to *you*? Choose your most important needs in each broad area (survival needs, emotional needs, fulfilment needs) and prioritise them. The aim is to get a clear understanding of your individual needs.

For the sake of this exercise, the three survival needs (food, water and shelter) have been assumed as being common for everyone! However, it is important to remember that meeting these very basic needs can have a very powerful effect upon our behaviour.

This may be quite a challenging task, and I encourage you to take as much time as you wish to complete it. It is perfectly acceptable to return to this exercise on several occasions.

Survival Needs		
FOOD More food Money for food Healthier food	WATER	SHELTER Bigger home Garden/land Relocation Money for rent/ mortage

Emotional Needs			
CONTROL	VARIETY	SIGNIFICANCE	CONNECTION
Assurance	Adrenalin	Acceptance	Adoration
Balance	Autonomy	Accomplishment	Attention
Be obeyed	Change	Achievement	Cherish
Correctness	Difference	Appreciation	Communication
Calmness	Excitement	Approval	Desire
Clarity	Freedom	Authority	Esteem
Commitment	Independence	Compliments	Friendship
Control	Stimulation	Flattery	Inclusion
Domination	Surprise	Honour	Love
Guarantee		Influence	Need
Management		Memorable	Sharing
Peace		Notice	Touch
Precision		Popularity	Understanding
Promises		Power	
Protection		Praise	
Safety		Thanks	
Security		Value	
Stability		Victory	
		Worthy	

Fulfilment Needs	
GROWTH	CONTRIBUTION BEYOND SELF
Achievement	Assistance
Autonomy	Campaign
Freedom	Duty
Fulfilment	Effect
Independence	Help
Liberation	Inspiration
Performance	Return
Reach	Return
Realisation	Satisfaction
Self-reliance	

This exercise should have given you a significant insight into the personal needs that you have and greater self-awareness than the average person.

You will be able to use this knowledge to enhance your performance in many areas of your life.

You are now aware of why you choose to do many of the things you do, and you will be able to use the knowledge you have to power you on your way to achieving some stretching new goals.

Your Values

As you were working in the fulfilment needs area, you will have started to move into another significant area of personal understanding – your values.

Generally speaking, when you meet one of your needs, you feel satisfied. When you get one of your values expressed you will feel fulfilment. Fulfilment is an inner feeling that goes beyond happiness or satisfaction. It is the feeling of being totally you.

The area of meeting fulfilment needs can be thought of as a crossover from satisfying needs to fulfilling values. Needs and values are different, although there is inevitably some degree of overlap.

So what are values? Your values reflect what is important in life, how you see the world and what you believe in. They can be thought of as your principles and standards. Values are also sometimes described as activities, behaviours and preferences that you are naturally drawn to.

By understanding what is most important to you and by setting and achieving goals based upon this, you will be able to achieve something that most people only hope to do – live your life the way you want to.

Being clear about what your values are allows you to take your life in a direction that will be fulfilling not only mentally and emotionally but also spiritually – if this is something that is important to you.

It is worth spending time to determine and clarify what your values are so that you can orientate your goals and your life around them.

Below is a list of possible values. Take some time to consider the values that you feel are most important to you. You may wish to consider values that are not on the list. Again, the list is not exhaustive, they are just suggestions. Please feel free to add any other examples of values that may occur to you.

Which of these values matter to you? Choose your ten most important values and prioritise them. The aim is to get a sense of your most important values in life.

Do not be overly concerned if this proves to be a challenging task.

Very few people will take the time to complete an exercise such as this. Those that do will find that it makes a significant contribution and adds depth to their understanding of themselves.

You can then ensure that what you do on an ongoing basis is orientated around and reflects your values. This brings great clarity and increase fulfilment; it enables you 'to keep the main thing the main thing'.

Understanding what is important to you allows you to focus on what is important. It allows you to make informed choices about what you want to do, and also what you don't want to do.

Values		
Accomplish	Educate	Loyalty
Achieve	Elegance	Mastery
Acquire	Encourage	Nurture
Adventure	Enlighten	Organise
Alignment	Evolution Excellence	Patience
Assist	Exhilaration	Persuade
Attain	Experience	Play
Attract	Family	Pleasure
Authenticity	Fitness	Positivity
Balance	Freedom	Possibility
Beauty	Fun	Potential
Bliss	Gratitude	Power
Care	Guide	Purpose
Career	Health	Respect
Catalyse	Humour	Risk
Challenge	Imagination	Serve
Coach	Impact	Simplicity
Compassion	Improve	Speculation
Communication	Influence	Spirituality
Community	Inform	Strengthen
Contribution	Inspire	Support
Courage	Instruct	Teamwork
Create	Integrity	Thrill
Curiosity	Invent	Touch
Danger	Lead	Truth
Dare	Learn	Uncover
Design	Love	Uplift
Discover		Win

Very few people ever engage in this process of understanding what is important to them. It can take a considerable amount of time to get a full understanding of your individual needs and values, indeed you may discover that you refine and update your lists on an ongoing basis. I would certainly recommend that, at the very least, you review them on an annual basis.

Once you have established your needs and values, you will be able to focus on these as the motivating factors for your most important goals.

Having built the firm foundation of identifying, clarifying and prioritising your personal needs and values, we can move onto the next stage of the goal-setting process.

The Power of What?

> 'If you don't know what you want,
> you aren't going to get it.'
> **DR BOBBIE SOMMER**

S.M.A.S.H. your goals

The process that follows is recommended when setting your outcome goal (what it is you want to achieve). This process will then be supported with performance and process goals.

The mnemonic **S.M.A.S.H.** stands for:

> **S**pecific
> **M**easurable
> **A**chieveable
> **S**tretching
> **H**armonious & Holistic

By following each of these steps you will be able to set your goal (the what?) in the most effective manner possible.

Specific

It is important to know specifically what it is that you want. Your goal must be stated in the positive: what you do want rather than what you do not want.

Research demonstrates that explicit, specific and numerical (where appropriate) goals are most effective in facilitating behavioural change. If you want to see personal performance improvements, then you must set specific and measurable goals.

You do not go shopping in a supermarket with a list of all the things you don't want. Do the same when setting your goals. It is understood that the unconscious mind (everything you are not thinking about with your conscious mind at this moment) cannot process negative commands.

In order to think of something you do not want, you have to think and focus your attention upon the very thing you do not want to happen.

It is also theorised that the information flows into the unconscious mind almost instantly whereas the conscious mind will take a few seconds longer to process something.

So by the time your conscious mind has processed your goal to stop doing something (e.g. smoking) your unconscious mind has already processed the concept of smoking in order to make sense of the goal. Your unconscious mind is now focused on the very thing you want to stop doing!

Measurable

How will you know when you have achieved your goal? What will it look, sound and feel (taste and smell) like?

If, for example, you set a goal to 'get more money' and someone gave you a £1 coin, would you have achieved your goal? Exactly how much more money is 'more money'?

Create a sensory-rich, specific goal. The more sensory specific data you can include, the more your brain has to lock on to.

It can also be important to set specific dates by which you will achieve your goals. These dates will provide a reminder and create a sense of positive urgency.

The exception to setting dates is where the outcome goal is so challenging you could not realistically assign a date!

Although the common goal-setting wisdom is to assign dates to goals, I believe it can also be important to set goals that are way beyond what you think is currently possible.

Some of the great achievers report that when they set some of their most ambitious goals, they had no idea of how they were going to achieve them. The 'how' came along later.

I recommend a balanced approach to goal-setting and a few 'shoot for the stars' goals can form part of your goal-setting process. As the saying goes, if you shoot for the stars you might just end up over the moon.

Achieveable

Is the ability to achieve and maintain your goal something you have control over?

If your goal relies on other people acting or behaving in a certain way, then this is not under your control. Your goal must be about what *you* are going to do.

Stretching

Is your goal challenging enough?

Research demonstrates that specific and challenging goals lead to a higher level of performance than easy goals.[30]

There is a direct relationship between goal difficulty and task performance. The more difficult the goal, the better the performance will be.

Whilst care should be taken to ensure that goals are difficult/challenging and realistic (lack of realism may lead to failure and frustration), laboratory-based studies have shown positive relationships between goal difficulty and performance, even in the case of unattainable goals.[31]

Harmonious & Holistic

Is there anything you might lose as a result of achieving your goal?

How can you achieve your goal and maintain the benefits of how things are now?

This identifies the benefits in your current situation. If there were no benefits to things being the way they are you would probably have made some changes already. For example, achieving your goal may mean you have to put some additional effort in, and this may impact on your leisure time. By being aware of any downsides of setting your goal, you can find creative ways

---

30 Locke, E.A. (1968) Towards a theory of task motivation and incentives, *Organisational Behaviour and Human Performance*

31 Locke, E.A., and Latham, G.P. (1990) *A Theory of Goal Setting and Task Performance*, Prentice-Hall

to achieve your goal and maintain the current benefits. This will help to prevent the phenomena known as 'self-sabotage'.

Having done the exercise on identifying your most important personal needs and values, you will be in a good position to ensure that working towards and achieving your goals will bring you much satisfaction and fulfilment. In this way, you are unlikely to 'self sabotage'.

It is recommended that you set goals for *all* important areas of your life. The process of defining specifically what you want in all key areas will ensure that appropriate effort is spent on each area and that one (or more) key areas do not suffer at the expense of another.

It is hoped that following this 'holistic' goal-setting process will make a significant contribution to the balance of your life. It would be detrimental if you achieve one of your goals only to discover that it has had serious consequences in other areas of your life.

Areas of your life in which you may wish to set goals include:

- **Family/Significant relationships:** These relate to your family in whatever sense you choose to define it, plus your relationship with your spouse or partner if you have one.

- **Home:** This relates to where you live or where you want to live. It can include work you would like to do to your home and garden.

- **Car:** If this is something that is important to you then you might like to set a goal to own a particular make or model of car.

- **Social life/Friends:** This relates to relationships outside your family and other significant relationships.

- **Physical/Health:** This could include physical fitness, diet, health care, recovery from injury etc.

- **Career/Work/Business:** This could include your career plan, finding a new job, increasing your pay, starting or growing your own business etc.

- **Financial:** This could relate to clearing debt, investing, setting a household budget etc.

- **Personal Development/Learning:** This could relate to education, attending courses, reading educational books (which you are doing right now), listening to motivational recordings etc.

- **Spiritual:** This is about how you relate to the area of spirituality or religion. If you are atheist or agnostic then you may have a different interpretation for this area or indeed ignore it altogether.

- **Leisure:** This includes hobbies and interests, holidays, relaxation and fun!

- **Community:** This would include things you do to contribute to your local (or wider) community, however you choose to define this.

I appreciate that this may seem a lot to think about. Although it can seem so at first, people usually report that after completing this exercise they gain tremendous clarity and focus about what they want to achieve in all of the important areas of their life.

This allows them to get good focus on the specific things that they want to achieve, and ensure they have a sensible balance across the key areas of their life. In my experience you tend to get more of what you focus on, so it is important to make sure you are focussing in the right areas.

The Power of How?

> 'Once you have strong enough reasons 'why',
> you will be able to work out the 'how'.'
> **TONY ROBBINS**

Once you have established your goal, the *'what'* you want to achieve, by following the above process, you can then focus on *'how'* you are going to do it.

I recommend that these stages are done separately, and that you work on setting your goal before doing any work on how you are going to achieve it. If the practicalities and challenges of how you are going to achieve your goal are allowed to interfere or pollute the goal-setting process then this may damage its effectiveness.

A formula for goal-setting and goal achievement

Know what you want

This is achieved by following the goal-setting process in the previous chapter.

Identify as many strategies to achieve your goal as possible

Techniques such as brainstorming can be used to generate as many as possible ways to achieve the desired goal. These can then be refined into plans of action.

> 'One choice is no choice, two choices is a
> dilemma, three choices is a start...'
> **DR RICHARD BANDLER**

The importance of setting performance and process goals must be emphasised here. These focus the individual onto the task-relevant strategies and procedures needed to achieve the desired performance levels for outcome goal achievement.

Too much focus on the outcome goal can be distracting and cause one to worry about attaining the goal and not attend sufficiently to the task-relevant strategies involved.

Plot a series of dated sub-goals along the way to your outcome goal.

For example, when planning to run my first marathon I set my outcome goal: 'To complete the marathon in less than four hours with a secondary outcome goal of just managing to finish the event'!

I then set a series of staged performance goals to gradually increase the length of my training runs to get me ready for the date of the event. I also set some process goals that I used to focus my attention upon when on training runs. These included for example, using the 'fartlek' speed play method that incorporates different paced running intervals.

It is useful to keep goals fluid and dynamic. There is a difference between flexibility and procrastination. You may need to revise your action steps and the date you will achieve each one by. These measurements are intended to be guide posts and not whipping posts!

Take action

Without focused action being taken, nothing is going to happen. Measure the results of your action against your performance and process goals.

Pay attention to the results you are getting

Once you have taken action, pay attention to what happens, whatever happens; if you take action you will get some sort of result. It may not be the result you want, but taking action will also give you more experience and information that you can use to enhance and enrich your plan.

> 'There is no failure - only feedback'
> **NLP MAXIM**

Be behaviourally flexible - if what you are doing is not working then change your approach

When you set your goals initially, you do so based upon the knowledge and experience you have at the time. When you take action towards achieving your goals, and pay attention to the results you are getting, you will gain new knowledge and experience.

> 'Insanity is doing the same thing and hoping for a different result.'
> **ALBERT EINSTEIN**

It is perfectly acceptable, and indeed recommended, to incorporate what you have learned and alter, tweak, revise or reset your goals based upon what you have discovered.

This is rather like going on a journey by car and following the route you think will get you to where you want to go. As you proceed on your journey, you will gather more information that will help you to re-plan your route.

You would not carry on your previous route if you found it was not getting you to where you wanted to go, would you? You would be flexible in your approach and as a result would get where you want to go.

> 'If what you are doing isn't working, do *anything* else!'
> **NLP MAXIM**

What happens when I set goals?

Setting goals is one of the most important skills you will ever learn. When you set goals you are gaining the advantages of one of the most powerful and proven methods to enhance and improve your personal performance and achievement – in all areas of your life.

A series of well-defined and structured goals will give you direction, motivation and a sense of personal control of your life. Goals put you into the driving seat.

The power of goal-setting comes from answering the two most important questions anyone can ask:

> 1. What do you want?

The things you want to achieve, your outcome goals.

> 2. What do you *really* want?

The needs that will be satisfied and the values that will be fulfilled by the goals.

A series of well-considered goals around what is most important to you, empower you with a strong sense of congruence. Congruence means that your thoughts, words and actions will be aligned with each other. This congruence or alignment will keep you focused on what it is you want to achieve and prevent distraction.

When your goals are well thought through, you will have a definite sense of purpose. Your goals and actions will be right for you. This will make what you do more fulfilling and satisfying. In this way your unique contribution can manifest itself through what you choose to do.

'There should be truth in thought, truth in speech and truth in action.'
MAHATMA GHANDI

Goal-setting Exercise

Now it is time to develop your very own list of goals. This exercise will guide you through a comprehensive and robust goal-setting process. By the time you have finished, you will have a well thought through set of goals that cover all the key areas of your life.

All aspects of your life are interrelated and there is considerable benefit in ensuring that you have a balanced set of goals that contain all of these key aspects.

In this way, no area of your life will be ignored for the sake of another. It is important to have balance so that your goals for one key area will be supported and not contradicted by a set of goals for other areas of your life.

Please follow the step-by-step process and take as much time as you need to complete the entire goal-setting process. You do not have to do it in one session. Work at whatever pace is right for you.

Step 1: Define Your Needs

Take the list of needs you identified earlier and review them. Ensure you have identified the key needs that you have in each of the following areas:

- **Survival Needs:** Food, Water, Shelter
- **Emotional Needs:** Control, Variety, Significance, Connection
- **Fulfilment Needs:** Growth, Contribution beyond self

Create a list of your needs on a separate piece of paper headed 'My Needs'.

Step 2: Define Your Values

Take the prioritised list of values that you created earlier. Review it to make sure you are satisfied with it. Make sure it also is listed on a separate piece of paper headed 'My Values'.

Step 3: Brainstorm Your Goals

Spend at least 20 minutes brainstorming all the things you might want to have, do or be. Use as many sheets of paper as you like and let your imagination flow. Do not think too much about each idea as it comes to you. Just keep writing down ideas as fast as they come.

Step 4: Group Your Goals into Key Areas

Take a separate piece of paper for each of the following areas and write at the top of each sheet:

- Family / Significant Relationship Goals
- Home Goals
- Car Goals
- Social Life / Friends Goals
- Health Goals
- Career / Work / Business Goals
- Financial Goals
- Personal Development / Learning Goals
- Spiritual Goals
- Leisure Goals
- Community Goals

Then transfer the goals from your brainstorm session onto the relevant sheet of paper. If you do not have goals for a particular area then you might like to consider if you should.

However, it is perfectly OK not to have goals for some of the above areas. Feel free to ignore any areas that are not relevant to you.

Step 5: Determine Your Top Ten Goals

From your various sheets of goals, decide on your top 10. What are the 10 most important goals that you want to achieve in your life?

Capture these on a sheet of paper titled 'My Top 10 Goals'

Then put each of these goals through the S.M.A.S.H. process we discussed earlier. Make sure that each goal meets the S.M.A.S.H. criteria.

Take a separate piece of paper for each of these ten goals. Each goal should have the following information:

- Affirmative goal statement that is positive and present tense, e.g. 'I am the number one salesperson at my company!' or 'I am the national champion!'
- Goal evidence: How will you know when you have achieved your goal?
- Picture of your goal: Having a picture or photograph that depicts or reflects your goal is very powerful. Do not be concerned if your drawing ability is not good; you can use photographs out of magazines instead. Any drawing or illustration is better than no drawing or illustration. The unconscious mind can easily understand pictures and even badly drawn representations of a goal can be powerfully received.
- Date by which you will achieve your goal. Only include a date for goals you know you will be able to achieve within a specific timescale. For some of your 'shoot for the stars' goals, leaving them without a date is acceptable. The act of setting a lofty goal can have powerful effects. You may not have any idea of how or when you are going to achieve some of your goals. Do not concern yourself about this. The act of setting the goal is a powerful start.
- What needs does achieving this goal satisfy? Add the relevant needs from your 'My Needs' sheet
- What values does achieving this goal fulfil? Add the relevant values from your 'My Values' sheet.
- What is your action plan to achieve each goal? What steps do you need to take? By what date will you have taken each step?

Step 6: Determine Your Top Three Goals for the Next 12 Months

Choose your three most important goals for the next 12 months or so. For each of these, make sure you have put them through the process outlined above.

Create an action plan for your top three, most immediate goals and then… start taking action. Then don't stop until you have achieved them!

Congratulations on having spent the time and effort to determine goals that are important to you. A well thought through and balanced set of goals for your life is something only a small percentage of the population have.

The benefits you will receive as a result of making the commitment to achieve this can be significant. By setting goals you will discover that your performance improves in many areas of your life.

May I wish you the very best luck with achieving all of your goals.

As you set about achieving your goals please remember the story of the Olympic champion who was asked if he was lucky to achieve what he had achieved.

'Yes,' he said, 'I am lucky and do you know what, the harder I work the luckier I seem to get!'

"I Will" - How to Develop Your Self-Confidence

> 'We lead our lives as it is imagined in our minds.'
> **WILLIAM JAMES**

Why is Self-Confidence important?

A consistent finding in psychological research is a direct correlation between self-confidence and success. A study of over 700 athletes from 23 different sports concluded that elite performers had higher and more stable levels of self-confidence. The conclusion was that confidence was a major differentiating factor between elite and non-elite performers.[32]

High self-confidence leads to individuals selecting more difficult goals and having greater commitment to achieving these goals once they have been set. Further research suggests that when in stressful situations, people with lower self-confidence will tend to give up more readily and experience greater anxiety.[33] If you want to achieve your full potential, ensuring that you have developed your self-confidence to its fullest extent is an important priority.

What is Self-Confidence?

Self-confidence can described as a 'global' trait that accounts for overall performance optimism and attitude, but can also relate to a perception about one's ability to perform specific skills.

---

32   Mahoney , M.J. (1987) Psychological skills and exceptional athletic performance, *The Sports Psychologist*
33   Bandura, A (1982) Self–efficacy mechanism in human agency, *American Psychologist*

This perceived ability to perform specific skills is often referred to as self-efficacy, or situation specific self-confidence. Self-efficacy can be defined as your confidence in succeeding at a given task at a given time.

Optimism is strongly related to confidence. Optimism is a tendency to expect the best possible result or to focus on the most positive/hopeful aspects of any situation. The propensity to look for opportunities to grow, develop, win or excel regardless of the circumstance is vital to personal success.

When the three elements of self-confidence, self-efficacy and optimism are combined, they make up a very powerful 'I Can Do It!' belief that is both global and specific.

Confidence is often confused with arrogance. It is true that certain confident individuals are outspoken, loud, abrasive and brash. Muhammad Ali would be an example.

However, many quieter and more respectful individuals are every bit as confident. You can be a highly confident individual without being conceited or arrogant.

A well-developed sense of self-confidence and a positive 'Can Do' attitude is a very useful, practical and healthy thing to possess.

How you can develop unshakeable Self-Confidence

Whatever your current level of self-confidence, the inspiring news is that you can improve and enhance it. People who are confident have *developed* their confidence. As a result of developing their confidence they will think about themselves in a different way from those who lack confidence.

If you wish to enhance and strengthen your self-confidence then you need to understand that the mind can, and must, be disciplined in a similar way that the physical body is disciplined by physical training. Your mind is not automatically going to support you in what you want to achieve. It can and must be trained to think effectively.

Our thoughts affect how we are feeling and this affects our actions. Inappropriate thinking often leads to negative feelings and poor performance. Appropriate thinking leads to positive and enabling feelings and good performance.

Confidence is the result of specific thinking habits and when these habits are practised until they become natural and automatic, significant benefits can be realised.

We will explore the area of thinking and mind in further detail. It may come as some surprise to you that you have not one mind but two. Or, to be more precise, two spheres of activity within one mind. These minds are called the conscious mind and the unconscious mind. It is important that you understand the differences between the two.

Your Conscious Mind

Your conscious mind is your reasoning, objective level of mind. It is the mind you are aware of when you are fully awake. Its role is to take in information, analyse it and decide if some action should be taken. It is the mind that you consciously 'think' with.

If your conscious mind accepts some information as valid, it is transferred immediately to the unconscious mind that then processes and files it. For example, as a small child you did not know that a flame would burn your skin. Either from actually burning yourself or by observing the terrified reactions of your parents as you moved towards the flame, your conscious mind realised that: 'flame equals pain. Do not touch flames.' This information would then be passed to the unconscious mind that accepts it *without question.*

Your Unconscious Mind

Your unconscious mind is your automatic, subjective level of mind. It operates below your level of conscious awareness. It maintains all essential life-maintenance systems such as digestion, breathing, eyelid blinking etc.

It can be likened to a vast memory bank. All your life experiences pass through the conscious mind and are stored in the unconscious mind. All experiences are stored, be they positive or negative. These experiences are not just passively stored but are actively stored. This stored data persistently floods your conscious mind with feelings and emotions that affect your thoughts.

The famous hypnotherapist Ormond McGill has said that each of these memories and experiences stored in the unconscious mind are 'forming a thread in the texture of our personality, the total of these impressions being the nature of the individual'.

The role of the unconscious mind is to make sure that you always think, behave and perform in a manner consistent with the information you have accepted as true with your conscious mind.

Your unconscious mind is concerned with your survival. It maintains a constant vigil. It never sleeps. No psychologist or scientist has ever been able to give a full description of its abilities or activities. It is universally accepted as a very powerful force in our lives.

Your unconscious mind concentrates on maintaining what is known as your 'world view'. This is your unconscious mind's map of the world. Your world view is a powerful survival tool. For example, your world view tells you that if you step off a cliff you will hurt or kill yourself. This aspect of your world view protects you from danger by preventing you from having to experience the danger of falling every time you are on a cliff top.

Once your unconscious mind has established a coherent world view it is reluctant to allow any data in that may conflict with it. It will therefore accept or reject information depending upon other information that it holds.

In the process of growing up, we will all have experienced our share of 'positive' and 'negative' events. All of these events are stored in your unconscious data bank. You have probably consciously forgotten many of the actual incidents, but their unconscious effect continues.

If a new idea is now presented to you, you will either reject or accept it depending upon your stored data. In addition to this your unconscious mind influences your emotions, thoughts and attitude. You may not be consciously aware of this, but it does have a powerful influence over your life.

It is important to realise that the unconscious mind does not rationalise. It does not enter into logical debate. It just controls. Your unconscious mind does not necessarily work to provide what is logically best for you. It works to provide what its stored data tells it is best for you.

It does not care if you are 'happy'. It does not understand happy. It does not think in the conscious sense of the word. It instructs automatically, based upon its stored data. If the data it holds is negative, then it could actually be working against what you desire.

Your Self-Image

We have seen how the unconscious mind has stored every experience of your life in its vast data bank. This data contributes towards what can be described as your self-image.

Your self-image is quite simply the image you have of yourself that you believe is true.

As you were growing up, your unconscious mind has stored all the experiences, emotions, criticisms, praise and so forth in its data bank. This has all been instrumental in forming your self-image. It is the sum total of all of your past experiences, both good and bad, plus all the thoughts you have accumulated throughout your life.

Your self-image is made up of thousands and perhaps even millions of mini self-images. You will have a self-image of how good or bad you are at a huge range of activities – sport, public speaking, cooking, making love, reading, writing, making money and so on. Then you will have a huge number of self-images about how intelligent you are, how popular you are, how funny you are and so on. You have a mini self-image for every single aspect of your life.

Our early experiences as children continue to affect our self-image when we are adults; our parents and other people have had a lot of influence over our self-image. Many of these people may have had poor self-images themselves. These influences can be passed on from parent to child and can be useful or not depending upon what they are.

When you enter into any situation in your adult life, your mind instantly compares it to the information it has stored in its data bank. Your self-image therefore has considerable control over your life. As the psychologist William James put it: 'We lead our lives as it is imagined in our minds.'

Much of how you feel about yourself is the result of a self-image (or more specifically a collection of mini-self images) that you probably haven't been consciously aware of. Your thoughts, feelings and behaviour will reflect your self-image. Much of your conscious thought is the result of the content of your unconscious mind and your self-image.

It would therefore be useful to have a healthy self-image and hold data in your unconscious mind that supports you in a positive manner. As Brian Tracy states in *The Psychology of Achievement*: 'What you think – you are'.

Quite simply, if you change your thoughts you can change your life. Your life up to today has been the result of your thoughts – both conscious and unconscious. If you change these thoughts now, in the present, you can change your life in the future.

The past does not necessarily equal the future. You can design the future you want. By changing the data stored in your unconscious mind and by enhancing your self-image you can make significant and positive changes to your confidence and success.

Let us now take a look at specific ways to do this.

Misconceptions about Self-Confidence

A useful place to start is to look at some of the misconceptions or limiting beliefs that exist about confidence:

Either you are confident person or you are not

Some people believe that confidence is something that comes naturally to some people and not to others; it is in some way an inherited trait.

High levels of self-confidence do not occur randomly. Self-confidence is the result of thinking positively and constructively on an on-going basis. People who develop high levels of self-confidence retain the positive benefits from successful experiences and de-emphasise their less successful experiences. Confidence is gained in exactly the same way as other skills – through practice and repetition of the desired skill.

Confident people are arrogant

Whilst we may all be familiar with confident individuals who are outspoken and brash, it is crucial to realise that you can be confident without being conceited or arrogant. It could be suggested that those who are truly confident have no need to demonstrate it with brash or arrogant behaviour.

Making mistakes/losing damages confidence

The truth is that we are human, and part of being human is making mistakes from time to time. Some people respond to mistakes by weakening their confidence. Other people continue to build their confidence despite any failures. They choose to seek the learning from any mistake and use it to get improvements in their performance.

Confidence is the result of how you think, what you choose to focus upon and how you choose to respond to the events that occur in your life.

There are three specific areas upon which you should focus to develop your self-confidence.

Understand that how you think affects how you perform

It is widely understood that the thoughts we have regarding our ability, the challenges we face and the environment in which we are operating determine to a large extent how we feel about ourselves at any one moment. For example thinking, 'I can do this' will result in increased feelings of confidence. Thinking, 'I can't possibly do this' will result in a loss of confidence.

These feelings directly affect performance. It is proven, scientific fact that these thoughts and feelings cause verifiable changes in muscle tension, blood flow, hormone production and attentional focus. For example, thoughts of failure lead to anxious feelings and an increase in overall muscle tension. If the wrong muscles are tense at the wrong time, then sporting performance, for example, will be adversely affected.

So to increase your confidence, direct your thoughts and focus your attention onto aspects of yourself, the challenges you face and the environment you are in that will produce powerful, confident feelings. These will in turn improve your performance.

Develop honest self-awareness

Your aim is to develop control over your thoughts and feelings. In order to do this you must be honest with yourself.

Honestly ask yourself the question: 'Am I now thinking in a way that will give me the very best chance of success?' If your thinking is poor you have to win 'the battle' with yourself as well as your real opponent. People with high levels of confidence have succeeded in winning this battle.

As Plato said, 'The first and best victory is to conquer self. To be conquered by self is, of all things, the most shameful and vile.'

Develop an optimistic outlook

We will all have a habitual 'style' that we use to interpret events in our life. This is sometimes described as being either an optimist or a pessimist.

This habitual style of interpreting events is developed in childhood and according to psychological theory stems directly from your view of your place in the world, whether you think you are valuable and deserving or worthless and hopeless.

The achievement of any significant success in any area of life will inevitably result in some obstacles and set-backs. These need to be responded to with determination and optimism if you wish to maintain high levels of confidence.

This does not mean that you ignore your mistakes or adopt a totally unrealistic view of your abilities. Rather it means looking at any mistakes and failures rationally and using them as positive aids to improving your performance.

Mistakes and shortcomings can make a very powerful contribution to performance improvement, providing that the focus is on how you can use what you have learned to improve.

'A real optimist is aware of problems but recognises the solutions, knows about difficulties but believes they can be overcome, sees the negatives but accentuates the positives, is exposed to the worst but expects the best, has reason to complain but prefers to smile.'
WILLIAM JAMES

Self-Efficacy Theory

The theory of self–efficacy referred to earlier offers some interesting methods of self-confidence or self-efficacy enhancement.

According to the theory, efficacy expectations (i.e. one's belief that a certain level of performance can be attained) are predicted by four factors which are, in descending order of importance:

1. Performance Accomplishments

Previous performance accomplishments represent the most powerful effects upon self-efficacy since they are based on 'personal mastery' experiences. The more positive the experience was, the higher the self-efficacy. If you have been successful before you will be inclined to think you can be so again.

2. Vicarious Experience

This refers to the information you can derive from seeing others perform the task, skill or challenge in question. This can be a particularly important source of efficacy information if you lack experience of the task at hand. Seeing someone else successfully perform can inspire you to believe that it is possible that you can do likewise.

> 'What one man can do another can do.'
> **ANTHONY HOPKINS, *THE EDGE***

3. Verbal Persuasion

This refers to persuasive techniques used by yourself or by others (e.g. a coach or teacher) in order to positively manipulate behaviour. These techniques may include verbal encouragement ('You can do it!') and feedback.

4. Emotional Arousal

This refers to your appraisals of your emotional arousal as opposed to your actual physiological states. Thus it is your appraisal or interpretation of your physiological response that will contribute to efficacy expectations.

One person can interpret feelings of nervousness as negative and this will affect their feelings of self-efficacy. Another person may interpret the same feelings as a productive part of getting themselves sharpened up mentally to compete effectively, with the result that their feelings of self-efficacy are enhanced. We will explore this concept in greater detail later in this section.

Specific techniques to enhance Confidence

What follows is a rich collection of techniques and tactics you can use to enhance your self-confidence and self-efficacy.

The Circle of Excellence

This is a simple but powerful technique that comes from the field of psychology known as NLP:

- Stand up and imagine a circle on the floor. Make it three feet in diameter and two feet in front of you. You can make the circle a bright colour if you choose.

- Now think back to a time when you felt very confident and on top of everything. If you cannot remember such a time, then make it up! You could also imagine how a favourite sporting personality or film star would feel. Imagine it fully. It does not matter how you create the feelings of confidence so long as you evoke a very positive and confident state.

- When you have fully accessed this positive state then step into the circle and fully experience what you are seeing, hearing, feeling, smelling and tasting. Step out of the circle just before the positive state peaks.

- Repeat this process again and this time once you have stepped into the circle and you are experiencing the positive state, press your thumb and forefinger together and say a positive trigger word to yourself. This can be any word you choose and examples would include 'Confident!', 'Powerful!', 'Winner!' Alternatively, imagine playing some of your favourite motivating music to yourself inside your head.

Although this exercise may seem somewhat strange at first, what is happening is that you are taking a positive and confident feeling and associating it with the imaginary circle and the thumb/finger squeeze and your positive trigger word/music.

This technique uses your brain's ability to swiftly associate one thing with another. When you have completed the Circle of Excellence exercise successfully your brain will associate feeling confident with the imaginary circle/thumb finger squeeze/ positive trigger word/music.

You can then put your Circle of Excellence anywhere, step into it and instantly trigger the feelings of confidence. Your Circle of Excellence is a portable resource that you can take anywhere.

Ha Breathing

One very powerful way to affect how you are feeling is to use breathing techniques.

Ha Breathing is a technique that increases personal energy, calmness and confidence. It is thought to have originated from Huna - the ancient teachings of the Hawaiian people. It has also been reported to have been practised in ancient China.

When doing Ha breathing, breathe from the diaphragm, this is at the bottom of your rib cage. With diaphragmatic breathing, your stomach goes in and out. This is a good way to check that you are breathing from your diaphragm.

This is how you do Ha breathing:

- Sit or stand comfortably, in a balanced posture with your feet flat on the floor.

- Breathe in deeply through your nose. When you breathe in your stomach should come out. If you put your hand on your stomach you will be able to feel when you are doing this correctly. As you breathe in, your lungs fill with air, your diaphragm moves down, and your stomach comes out.

- Exhale through the mouth making a long 'Haaaaaaaaaaa aaaaaaaaaaaaa' sound. The out breath should be twice as long as the in breath.

- Continue to Ha breathe for as long as you like. Some people choose to do two sessions of twenty minutes at the beginning and end of each day. Other people use it immediately prior to any important occasion when they need to be calm, balanced and confident. I personally use it prior to my public speaking engagements.

Thought Stoppage

The technique of thought stoppage provides a very effective method for eliminating negative or counterproductive thoughts.

The technique begins with you being aware of an unwanted thought and uses a trigger to interrupt or stop the undesirable thought. The trigger can be a word such as 'Stop!', 'Delete!' or you can use a physical action such as snapping the fingers or slapping a hand against your thigh.

The trigger action interrupts the pattern of negative thought and enables you to get into a more positive state of mind.

Another variation is to wear an elastic band around you wrist and every time you become aware of a negative thought pattern you snap the elastic band onto your wrist. The slight discomfort and pain conditions your brain to avoid the negative thoughts and to focus on more positive thoughts.

Reframing

Reframing is an effective way of dealing with negative perceptions of a situation and turning them to your advantage. Reframing is the process of creating alternative frames of reference or different ways of looking at the world.

Because the world is what we make it (due to the data stored in our unconscious mind) reframing enables us to transform what may appear to be a weakness or difficulty into a strength or possibility. We can do this by simply looking at it from a different point of view. We can find a different way of perceiving a situation in order to give it another interpretation.

It is important to recognise that reframing is not about denying or ignoring what you are experiencing. Instead with reframing you acknowledge what is happening and choose to use it to your advantage.

If you are about to participate in an important event or meeting you might say, 'I am feeling anxious and tense'. An effective reframe would be, 'I am feeling excited and my body is preparing itself to do well'.

As a professional speaker, I am only too familiar with feeling nervous about standing up and talking to large groups of people. It seems that no matter how often I speak before large groups I always feel 'nervous'. However, utilising my understanding of how the body and mind function, I reframe the feeling. I view it as my body and mind preparing themselves to give a splendid performance. I reframe the feeling so that it gives me 'the edge' that I need to be at my very best in front of a large group of people.

An interesting study that compared the mental preparation of teams of athletes in the 1996 Olympics who either achieved or failed to meet their medal goals, concluded that members of more successful teams were able to 'reframe negative events in a positive light'.[34]

Self-Talk

Self-talk is quite simply what you say to yourself. At this point it is worth stressing that talking to yourself will not result in you being locked away in a mental institution!

The vast majority of people engage in self-talk to a greater or lesser degree. You engage in self-talk at any time that you carry on an internal or external dialogue with yourself. Examples of self-talk would include giving yourself encouragement or interpreting what you are feeling or perceiving.

---

34   Greenleaf, C., Gould, D., Diffenbach, K., (2001) Factors Influencing Olympic Performance *Journal of Applied Sports Psychology*

The use of positive affirmations, such as 'I Can Do This!' repeated to oneself, are a powerful example of self-talk. Positive, personal and present tense affirmations when repeated to oneself regularly can transform your feelings of self-confidence.

Self-talk is a powerful way to enhance self-confidence and in a subsequent chapter the whole area of self-talk and the use of affirmations will be explored in considerable detail.

Self Hypnosis

What is hypnosis? There are many theories but, as with much of the research into the amazing capabilities of the human mind, no-one knows for definite.

It is usually agreed that hypnosis is a particular state of mind or state of awareness. In this state of mind the unconscious rather than the conscious mind is dominant.

Hypnosis is a method of inducing an unconsciously responsive state of mind.

Hypnotic suggestions can alter hypnotised subjects' heart rates, anaesthetise parts of the body, cause skin to blister when a hypnotised subject is touched with a piece of ice and told it is a piece of hot metal and, perhaps less dramatically, allow you to change *any* and *every* facet of your mind and personality.

The whole area of self-hypnosis will be dealt with extensively in a separate chapter.

What if you develop unshakeable Self-Confidence?

By now you will have realised that self-confidence is something that you can develop. You can take your current levels of self-confidence and transform them. In doing so, you will enable yourself to access more and more of your potential.

Every human being is a rich oasis of potential and talent. Having confidence in yourself and in your abilities will allow you to realise more and more of your potential in every area of your life.

The great American car manufacturer Henry Ford once said: 'If you think you can or think you can't you are probably right.'

What Mr Ford was saying was that it is important to not limit ourselves. A strong, healthy self-image, feeling good about ourselves and having confidence in ourselves and our abilities, allows us to make greater and greater use of our limitless potential.

I will repeat once more the wise words of William James: 'We lead our lives as it is imagined in our minds.'

Just imagine what your life will be like when you have used the knowledge you have gained in this chapter and transformed your confidence in yourself and your ability to do whatever you choose to do.

Get Going!

How to get (and stay) highly motivated

In this chapter we will be exploring the empowering area of motivation. I doubt that many readers of this book would disagree that motivation is important. The common wisdom is that to achieve almost anything people need to be motivated.

However, we need to dig a little deeper into the subject so that we can fully understand motivation and its importance.

Why is Motivation important?

The winning individual must be hungry for success. This hunger for success is their motivation. Motivation can be thought of as a psychological fuel that powers you towards success and achievement.

You need this psychological fuel because on the journey towards any significant success or achievement there may be obstacles and setbacks. It is very rare for anyone to achieve anything of any great significance without experiencing some problems, challenges or setbacks. Motivation is therefore required to overcome such challenges and to achieve what you want.

What is Motivation?

A dictionary definition of the word 'motive' is 'a factor or circumstance that induces a person to act in a particular way'. So let's explore some of the factors that contribute towards this.

Needs Motivation

Traditional psychological motivation theories attempt to explain people's behaviour in terms of their social and biological needs. In an earlier chapter we explored the area of goal-setting. The goal-setting exercise that you undertook invited you to explore your personal needs as part of this process.

The model of human needs that you were introduced to groups needs into three broad categories:

Survival Needs
- Food
- Water
- Shelter

Emotional Needs
- Control
- Variety
- Significance
- Connection

Fulfilment Needs
- Growth
- Contribution Beyond Self

Generally speaking when one of your needs is met, you feel a sense of satisfaction. The drive to get any of these needs met is a motivating factor.

Values Motivation

We also explored identifying your personal values. Values reflect what is important to you in life, how you see the world and that you believe in. When one (or more) of your values is met you will feel a sense of fulfilment and you are therefore motivated to do achieve this.

Motivating Goals

Having a set of clearly defined goals (the 'What You Want') supported by an identified and defined set of personal needs and values (the 'What You Really Want') will provide you with a very effective form of motivation.

When you understand the underlying motivations behind your goals – needs and values – and have a set of goals that are well thought through and balanced, you are far more likely to achieve them.

People who confuse the 'what you want' (the object or aim of their desires) with the 'what you really want' (the satisfaction or fulfilment they are really seeking) may continually seem to sabotage themselves. They almost become their own worst enemy. They often want something very badly but have not thought the reasons through fully and completely.

It is wise to check 'If I could have this now would I have it?' By paying attention to your response to this question you can explore any reservations you may have. Ensuring you have thought such areas through fully will protect against you becoming diverted from achieving your goal.

The achievement of any significant goal will usually require effort and work. You may have to give some things up in order to achieve this goal. Until you are fully committed to paying the price of achieving your goal, you may find that you undermine your very own efforts.

This undermining (or self-sabotage) can be an unconscious process, hence the reason to think through the things you want to achieve fully and completely. In this way you may find that you achieve what you want (and what you really want) more easily.

This will ensure that you are not 'your own worst enemy' – you will be your own best friend! You will be a friend who ensures that you achieve goals that bring real satisfaction and true fulfilment. Goals that achieve this will be truly motivational!

Having completed the goal-setting exercise you will be in a privileged position, which the majority of people never achieve, of having a clear focus and direction for your life and an understanding of what is important to you.

To add to the motivating foundation of a well considered and constructed set of goals, we shall now look at other practical theories of motivation that you can use.

Intrinsic and Extrinsic Motivation

Motivation can be:

- **Intrinsic:** This is sometimes referred to as an 'internal motivation'. Phrases that typify intrinsic motivation would be: 'I just did it because I wanted to' or 'I wanted to get the best out of myself'. When people are motivated to perform some activity for its own sake they are said to be intrinsically motivated.

- **Extrinsic:** This is sometimes referred to as 'external motivation'. Phrases that typify extrinsic motivation would include 'I have always dreamed of winning a gold medal', 'I wanted to be number one'. When people are motivated to perform some activity only to obtain some form of external reward, they are said to be extrinsically motivated.

Motivation is also described as being 'internal' or 'external'. As a professional speaker, I am frequently asked to speak at conferences and events. I am often asked to make a keynote speech to 'get people motivated' or to 'get everyone fired up'. In essence I am being asked to be a form of external motivation. Whilst I do not underestimate the power and impact of external motivation, I know that my real job as a speaker is to inspire people, to remind them of their own potential, to re-light or fan the flames of their internal fire so that they have a powerful source of internal motivation. External sources of motivation are not under the control of the individual and therefore cannot be relied upon.

I am often asked by participants at my seminars how they can maintain the motivated feelings they get from the seminar once it is finished. I reply that they need to provide their own motivation and not rely so heavily on external motivation. I also joke with them that they must be internally motivated people anyway because they have made the effort to attend the seminar in the first place.

The serious message contained within the joke is that everyone is capable of being a positive and self-motivated individual – they just may not yet realise it.

To return to the original definitions, although motivation can be intrinsic or extrinsic, it is less likely that anyone will maintain strong motivation in the face of setbacks and adversity if they do not possess high levels of intrinsic motivation.

Cognitive Evaluation Theory

One of the most commonly cited theories of intrinsic motivation is cognitive evaluation theory. The theory proposes that individuals have an innate need to feel personally competent and self-determining.

The theory predicts that specific events will increase intrinsic motivation only to the extent that they enhance an individual's perception of their competence and self-determination.

Conversely, if events lead to a reduction in a performer's perceptions of either their personal competence or their self-determination, the intrinsic motivation will be decreased. In the context of cognitive evaluation theory, self-determination is sometimes described in terms of a 'locus of causality'.

Individuals are described as having an internal locus (a position or point) of causality when they perceive their actions to have been initiated (caused) by themselves.

Individuals are described as having an external locus of causality when they perceive their actions have been initiated or forced upon them by events external to themselves. The perception of choice is the vital factor. The difference between the internal and external locus of causality can be thought of in terms of responsibility.

The power of taking responsibility

If you wish to maximise your potential as an individual then I would strongly recommend that you consider the area of responsibility closely.

Many people allow their motivation, attitude, and subsequent behaviour to be dictated by external circumstances. They will allow any number of factors – the day of the week, the weather, the behaviour of others, whether they are wearing a 'lucky' item of clothing, or the venue for their performance to affect them. The individual who takes responsibility for themselves chooses to maintain an internal locus of causality.

Responsibility can be thought of as 'Response Ability' or the *ability to choose your response.*

The person who has chosen to take full personal responsibility will never be at the whim of external circumstances or other people. They have chosen to take responsibility for themselves, their attitudes, their behaviour and their results.

This philosophy of taking personal responsibility for oneself may run contrary to much of the way that our society appears to operate. In society today many people expect someone else to take responsibility for them and their welfare. Cries of 'I am entitled!' and 'Someone ought to do something about this!' can often be heard.

The individual who chooses to take complete responsibility for themself may find that they are in something of a minority. However, they will not allow external circumstances to dictate how motivated they are feeling. They will take responsibility for being motivated themselves. This form of motivation is not at the whim of external forces, it is powered by an internal force of personal responsibility.

> ### THE CHALLENGE
> Let others lead small lives,
> But not you.
> Let others argue over small things,
> But not you.
> Let others cry over small hurts,
> But not you.
> Let others leave their future in someone else's hands,
> But not you.
> **JIM ROHN**

The famous American speaker and author Dave Pelzer has the following to say on the subject of personal responsibility:

> *I strongly believe that as a society we some time ago crossed a threshold at which a great number of individuals give up on themselves too easily. We have raised generations who not only look for others to rescue them on virtually every matter concerning their lives, but demand that others – whether parents, friends, employers or the government – immediately solve their problems to their liking. I learned as a child, shivering in my mother's garage the value of personal responsibility and opportunity'*

As a child Dave Pelzer suffered the worst ever recorded case of child abuse in the state of California. In his autobiography *A Child Called 'It'* he says:

> *If I learned anything from my unfortunate childhood it is that: there is nothing that can dominate or conquer the human spirit. How can you expect to be a good parent, an astute businessperson, or achieve your greatness if you do not focus and harness your inner potential?*

What I believe Dave Pelzer is saying is that we can choose to accept responsibility for ourselves, and our motivation, or we can choose to leave it to other people and external circumstances.

I find it inspirational that someone who had such an unfortunate start in life as Dave Pelzer can choose to take this level of responsibility for himself. I would encourage you to consider this philosophy for yourself.

Goal Orientations and Motivation

Psychological research has examined the effect that different goal perspectives have upon motivation. Goal perspectives refer to the comparisons individuals make in order to formulate their perceptions about how competent they are. This perception will have an effect upon their motivation.

- **Task Orientated** individuals make self-referenced comparisons in which their perception of their competence is based on improvements in their own level of performance at the task in question.

- **Ego Orientated** individuals will formulate their perceptions of confidence by comparison of their own ability against those of others.

Goal orientation researchers tend to denigrate ego orientations, but this does seem to be contrary to the anecdotal evidence - you are unlikely to be a sporting champion without wanting to beat your opponents.

Whilst there is little evidence that ego orientations per se have detrimental motivational consequences, the potential impact of challenging circumstances on an individual with an ego orientation might include lowered perceptions about their competence.

A combination of high task and high ego orientation would appear be the most positive blend from a motivational point of view.

Get motivated – stay motivated!

We have explored the importance having motivating goals that are well thought through and that both satisfy our needs and fulfil our values.

When these are combined with:

- The understanding you now have of the various elements of motivation.
- The vital importance of taking responsibility for yourself and your motivation

You have a very powerful force to ensure you are fully motivated on your journey to success and the realisation of your true potential.

Are You Tough Enough?

Developing your mental toughness

Many people participate in sport and the martial arts because it challenges them. People also choose to expose themselves to other forms of challenge such as taking on a new job or difficult work project. Challenges such as these enable us to develop ourselves as human beings.

I enjoy participating in challenges that allow me to develop and test myself. I recently took part in the 'Three Peaks Challenge'. This challenge involves climbing the three highest mountains in the United Kingdom (Ben Nevis in Scotland, Sca Fell Pike in England and Mount Snowdon in Wales) inside 24 hours. Within the 24 hour limit, as well as climbing all three peaks, you also have to travel the 500 or so miles between them, eating and snatching a little sleep on the move.

I was part of a four-man team who attempted this challenge. Three of us were climbing, with the fourth member of the team driving us between the peaks.

At 9am on a sunny Saturday in June we started to ascend the biggest mountain in the United Kingdom, Ben Nevis in Scotland. Such is the height of the mountain that we started our ascent in warm sunlight and finished it in a snow blizzard at the summit.

After approximately four and a half hours we were back at the base of Ben Nevis and began our journey from Scotland down to Scafell Pike in England. We arrived at the base of the mountain at about 6pm and it took the team about three and a half hours to climb up and down Scafell Pike. We then began our journey to Mount Snowdon in Wales.

We arrived at the base of Mount Snowdon at 3.30 in the morning. We had so far spent eight hours climbing and 10 and a half hours travelling. We were tired and our legs were feeling the effects of the two bouts of climbing. It was cold and the rain was lashing down.

Faced with the prospect of a further four hours climbing, one of our team gave up and decided to stay in the people carrier with our driver. Despite being a very fit individual he felt that he just couldn't face a four hour climb in the dark and rain. At that crucial moment he just didn't have the mental toughness to carry on and complete the challenge.

The remaining team member and I completed the three peaks challenge within the 24 hour time limit. Despite exploring 'alternative descent options' (some people call this getting lost!) we reached the base of Mount Snowdon at 7.30am on the Sunday morning.

If you want to achieve exceptional levels of performance in any field you will face tough challenges. You have to be able to cope with these challenges when they arise. You have to be mentally tough enough to face these challenges and to master them. This is why mental toughness is vitally important. If you have it you will succeed. If you don't have it you will fail.

Why is Mental Toughness so important?

Recent psychological research suggests that 'mental toughness' may be a more important factor for people who participate in combat sports -- for example, being able to beat their opponents -- than physical attributes such as strength and power.

Mental toughness enables you to cope better with the demands placed upon you and gives you the ability to remain determined, confident and in control under pressure. In sporting competition situations, mentally tough people have a significant psychological advantage over their opponents.

In a recent psychological survey, 82% of coaches rated mental toughness as *the* most important psychological attribute in determining success in combat sports.[35]

If you want to achieve exceptional levels of performance, a strong will, commitment and dedication iare essential. On the way to significant accomplishments you may encounter dif-

---

35   Gould, D., Hodge, K., Peterson, K., & Petlichkoff, L. (1987). Psychological foundations of coaching: Similarities and differences among intercollegiate wrestling coaches. *The Sport Psychologist*

ficulties, challenges and set-backs. This is where your mental toughness becomes of vital importance.

What is Mental Toughness?

Mental toughness can be defined as having a psychological edge that enables you to:

1. Cope better with the demands that achieving exceptional levels of performance places upon you.
2. To be more consistently focused, determined, confident and in control than other people.

In a nutshell, mental toughness gives you a psychological winner's edge. People who have developed high levels of mental toughness have superior control over themselves and their state of mind.

In competitive situations people who have developed their mental toughness will, quite simply, win more often than other people.

What makes someone mentally tough?

There are some key elements that define the psychological make-up of the mentally tough individual. These are:

Goal orientation

Individuals who are mentally tough possess an unshakeable belief in their ability to achieve their goals. You have to believe that you are capable of achieving the goals that you have set for yourself.

Mentally tough people keep themselves focused on their goals and can remain fully focused on key tasks in the face of personal life distractions. The mentally tough individual will have the ability to block out personal problems that may interfere with their performance. They would not allow their mind to wander onto personal issues at inappropriate moments.

Desire and motivation

The mentally tough individual will have an insatiable desire and internalised motive to succeed. The mentally tough individual has an overpowering desire to succeed. This motivation can be understood, and more importantly developed, using a variety of psychological strategies.

Focus and Concentration

The mentally tough individual will have the ability to remain fully focused in the face of distractions. They will not allow anything to interfere with their performance. In addition they will be able to regain focus and concentration should any surprising incidents, or events that are outside of their control occur.

If you want to be the best then you have to be fully focused on what you are doing.

Coping with anxiety and pressure

Top performers in any field of endeavour need to learn to cope with adversity. For example, it is not uncommon for sports people to have to deal with stress regarding such factors as physical injury and performance slumps.

Stress can be defined as a state in which some demand is placed upon the individual, who is then required to react in some way to that demand. In its simplest form, coping is the way individuals deal with these types of demands.

Elite performers generally seem able to control their anxiety and generate an appropriate state that enables them to perform at their very best for more of the time. They are often able to do this because they have been trained to use highly effective relaxation and coping strategies. These strategies are easy to learn and use.

Bounce-back

The ability to bounce back from performance setbacks is a characteristic of the mentally tough person. In addition the mentally tough individual will often actually use setbacks to create an increased determination to succeed. A combination of persistence, resilience and enhanced motivation allows mentally tough performers to see setbacks as a stage or process along the road to ultimate success.

Push back pain

Mentally tough individuals can push back the boundaries of physical and emotional pain. The mentally tough individual is able to push themselves through physically and mentally demanding circumstances by being determined to carry on.

Self-belief

Mentally tough individuals have an unshakeable self-belief that they possess unique qualities and abilities that make them able to perform at exceptional levels. This is not to be confused with arrogance – it is a form of strong self-belief that is required to overcome the challenges of reaching the very top.

We will all possess differing degrees of mental toughness which we can develop and improve.

Many of the key areas that contribute towards mental toughness are discussed in separate chapters (e.g. goal-setting, motivation, belief). This chapter aims to give you an insight into the psychological makeup of the mentally tough individual.

One key area that has been included in this chapter is the importance of having the ability to bounce back.

How to bounce back

As described earlier, people with high levels of mental toughness have superior control over themselves and their state of mind. One vital aspect of mental toughness is having the ability to bounce back from setbacks and failures.

On the path to exceptional levels of performance and mastery in your chosen field, it is inevitable that if you are challenging yourself and your abilities sufficiently you will face challenges and setbacks.

It will be your choice about how you wish to manage these situations. You could choose to get angry and frustrated with yourself, or to moan and whinge. Or you could choose to view such events as a positive and good thing. A positive and good thing - how can failure be a positive and good thing?

If you have chosen to achieve exceptional levels of performance and achieve mastery in your chosen field, you have made a long-term (perhaps even a lifetime) commitment to improving yourself and your abilities on an on-going basis. You have chosen to challenge, stretch and develop yourself. Without this you would not be growing.

It therefore does not make sense to get frustrated and angry with the very setbacks that you yourself have invited through your chosen commitment. You need to learn to welcome and even enjoy the challenges and the setbacks, for in this way you will truly learn.

What follows are some ways in which you can make the required mental shift with regard to bouncing back from failures and setbacks.

Replay the error positively

As soon as possible after making what you perceive as an error (it is important to focus on the fact that powerful learning often occurs after an error) imagine or mentally rehearse in your mind successfully completing the required task or move.

If you were to do the opposite and replay the failure inside your mind then you would be conditioning your mind to make failure the preferred pattern. Instead, replay a successful outcome. It is rather like gently reminding yourself of the outcome you want.

Using positive questions

The process of asking yourself questions is a very powerful technique for focusing the mind. From time to time my work involves being an executive coach for senior managers in businesses. The main focus of my coaching approach is asking questions. I use questions to get the person I am coaching to generate their own answers and solutions to what initially appear to be almost impossible to solve problems.

You can use the power of questions to very swiftly alter your mental state from perhaps frustration at failure to a more resourceful and positive state of mind.

For example, rather than saying nasty things to yourself and berating yourself for your perceived poor performance you could ask:

'How could I have performed differently?'

'What have I learned that will make me even more successful next time?'

'What is good about this?'

When you ask a question, your mind will always answer. You therefore need to be very careful about asking yourself the right sort of empowering questions. View each performance as a learning exercise and use positive questions to focus on the future and not the mistake.

You get more of what you focus on. Focus on errors and mistakes and you may get more of them. Focus on learning and success and you will get more of that.

Learn to be optimistic

According to psychological research, optimists and pessimists make different attributions for their success and failure. Optimists attribute success to factors that are permanent, pervasive and personal – 'I have worked hard'. Pessimists see success as caused by factors that are temporary and external – 'It was my lucky day'.[36]

Optimists see failure as temporary, specific or external – 'It's just the way my opponents were drawn'. Pessimists see failure as personal, permanent and pervasive – 'I never do well at tournaments with these rules'.

---

36 Seligman, M. (1991) *Learned Optimism*, Knopf

I am not endorsing some form of naive total optimism. A total optimist would have trouble seeing and correcting problems where their performance was poor.

Analysing a failure for its causes can be very powerful learning experience. It is however recommended for your continual self-improvement that you maintain a healthy balance between optimism and taking responsibility for your performance. Neither total optimism, nor total pessimism leads you to be able to use your failures to improve.

Maintain a healthy balance and remember to view any setbacks that occur as an inevitable part of pursuing any challenging and worthy goal. If it was easy to obtain, it probably wouldn't be worth having!

'It's not how far you fall – it's how high you bounce that matters.'
CHARLIE 'TREMENDOUS' JONES

How to control pain

Another key aspect of mental toughness that will be discussed in this chapter is the ability to push back or control pain. The world of sport and the martial arts is unique in seeing pain as not only a normal part of it but in some ways even desirable.

The popular phrase 'no pain – no gain', positions pain as something you must expect and indeed welcome in order to hone your body.

It is very important at this stage to clearly differentiate between the 'positive pain' of exertion and the 'negative pain' that could indicate that injury is about to, or already has happened. Apart from extreme survival situations, the use of mental power to ignore or reduce pain is, quite simply, stupid.

The famous mountaineer Joe Simpson who wrote the book *Touching the Void* used all of his mental strength to crawl off a mountain in Peru with a badly broken leg. He did this to save his life. If someone was to behave in this way in other circumstances, it would be foolhardy.

Negative pain can often be acute, intense or sharp and you must heed these messages from your body. Positive pain is the feeling of often intense discomfort that accompanies periods of very intensive effort.

During physical training we deliberately choose to put our system under stress so that it can subsequently recover and grow, e.g. in the case of weight training to gain strength and power.

Enduring positive pain can move you to the next level of performance and can increase your tolerance to pain. You can probably recall when an exercise or movement that you now perform with relative ease was difficult and painful.

Providing you are certain that you are experiencing the positive pain of exertion and not the negative pain of potential injury there are some methods of controlling it.

Reframe the pain

One method is to re-frame or re-interpret the pain. If you have ever had an injection from a doctor or nurse they may have said that 'you will feel a scratch'. This is done to lessen the concern you may have about how painful the injection will be.

In a similar way, rather than refer to or think about pain as pain you may wish to describe it as discomfort, heat, feeling a burn or working your body hard. In this way you are not processing the thought 'pain' and all the negative associations that this has for you. You are re-framing it into something more positive.

How is your opponent feeling?

If you are in a competitive sporting situation the principle of this idea is to take your focus of attention away from yourself and to focus upon how your opponent is feeling.

Ask yourself a series of questions to achieve this change in focus:

- How is my opponent feeling?
- How much pain is he feeling?
- How tired is he feeling?
- How does it feel for him?

In asking yourself these questions your focus of attention will be on your opponent and not yourself. This can lessen the level of pain and discomfort you are feeling.

Distract yourself

Marathon runner Paula Radcliffe uses distraction if she begins to feel discomfort during races. With each step she takes she counts a number. She starts at one and stops at 300. Then if required she starts from one again.

In this way she distracts herself from the discomfort. You can easily adapt this counting technique for yourself.

Set small manageable goals

The famous mountaineer, Joe Simpson, had to literally crawl down a mountain with a badly broken leg in order to save his own life.

Simpson was in extreme pain and kept on setting himself small goals. He would pick a spot in the distance, such as a particular boulder or rock, and give himself twenty minutes to crawl to reach it. He repeated this over and over again until he reached his base camp.

This is a powerful and useful technique that focuses your attention on shorter, achievable goals. This can make the pain or discomfort more manageable than contemplating persevering through an entire event or training session.

Chant a mantra

Later we will explore the use of self-talk in greater depth. For now let us understand how it can be used to help to control pain and discomfort.

The way to use the technique of self-talk to control pain is to continually chant a mantra to yourself either inside your own mind or out loud if circumstances permit.

Examples could be:

'Easy, easy, easy, easy.'

'Feeling good, feeling good, feeling good.'

'Power, power, power, power, power.'

Again this distracts your attention away from the pain and has the added benefit of saturating your mind with positive suggestions.

In the 1996 summer Olympics, American gymnast Kerri Strug won a gold medal after a near perfect vault on a badly sprained ankle. So bad was the sprain that after the event she had to be carried by her coach.

As Strug ran down the runway of the arena, she was in intense pain. She chanted to herself 'I will, I will, I will' and completed the near perfect vault.

Experts believe that such positive thinking and determination sparks the release of internal chemicals in the human body. For example, endorphins increase your tolerance to pain and improve co-ordination, noradrenaline liberates more energy to your muscles and improves concentration and dopamine makes things appear to have slowed down.

By using the above techniques in a sensible and responsible manner you will be able to reach new heights of performance excellence.

Once you have finished reading this book, you will understand each of the characteristics of the mentally tough individual and how you can use a variety of powerful psychological techniques and tactics to develop your mental toughness. Stay tough!

Are You In Control?

How to change how you are feeling in seconds with State Management

In this chapter we will be exploring the empowering concept of 'State Management' and how you can gain control of how you are thinking and feeling. We will also be looking at how you can instantly 'turn on' almost any state of mind that you want.

By the time you have finished this exciting section you will be able to instantly feel more confident, powerful, determined or motivated – any time you want! Now how is that for a promise?

We will also be exploring the ideal mental state for exceptional or even peak performance. You will discover how to get yourself 'into the zone' and achieve effortless performance.

Why you need to be able to manage your state

Our emotional, physical and mental states have a powerful influence on our behaviour and performance. Have you ever had the misfortune of meeting someone who has 'got out of bed on the wrong side'? Perhaps you have even experienced this sort of feeling yourself.

When people are emotionally and/or physically at a low ebb, we may describe them as being in 'a bit of a state'. We also know that in order to perform, or even to begin certain tasks successfully, we need to be in 'the right state of mind'.

So let us define 'state'. State can be described as the total ongoing mental and physical conditions from which a person is acting. It is a combination of all of the thoughts, emotions and physiology that are expressed at any given moment – our mental pictures, feelings, sounds, physical energy, posture and breathing.

Your state changes on a continual basis. Some states feel better than others and some are better states to be in if you wish to perform certain tasks successfully. Generalised states that might enable you to perform well could include confident, happy, calm or powerful. Generalised states that may not be so helpful could include confused, fearful, anxious or frustrated.

Psyching up and psyching down

Athletes are trained by sports psychologists to get themselves into an appropriate state of activation (readiness to perform) for the specific events in which they are they are competing. They may 'psych up' or 'psych down' as appropriate.

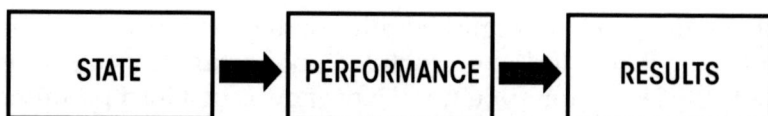

```
┌──────────┐      ┌──────────────┐      ┌──────────┐
│  STATE   │ ───▶ │ PERFORMANCE  │ ───▶ │ RESULTS  │
└──────────┘      └──────────────┘      └──────────┘
```

Have you ever tried to perform a delicate and complex task when feeling angry? Would it be useful to be able to exercise some choice over the states you experience?

What is State Management?

State Management is the ability to choose the most appropriate state at any given moment. State Management gives you the choice about the state you want to be in.

In order to perform to the best of your ability, the facility to choose and manage your own state, to be in the optimal mental, emotional and physical state for the specific task at hand is a useful skill.

By using a series of specific techniques you can alter your state at will, maintain positive states for longer periods and change negative states into more empowering ones. You will take control. When you are in an appropriate and resourceful state, your performance can improve.

How do I manage my states?

In order to answer this question it is appropriate to ask: 'What creates the state we're in?'

There are two main components that affect and (are affected by) our state:

- Your internal representations
- Your physiology

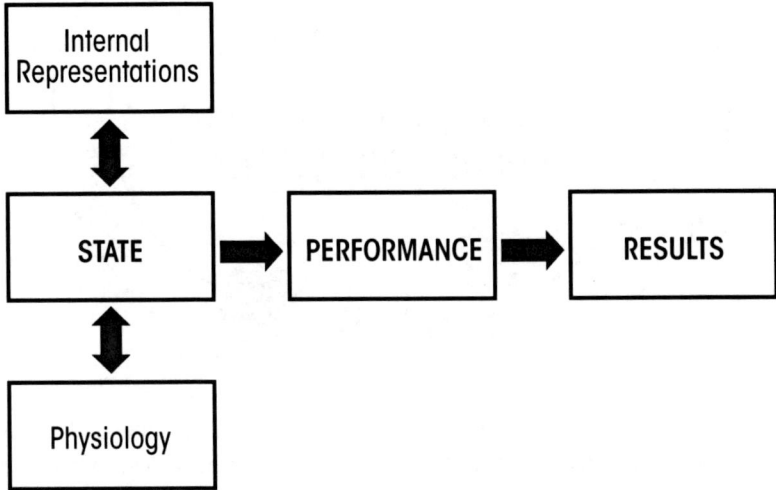

```
┌─────────────────┐
│    Internal     │
│ Representations │
└─────────────────┘
         ↕
┌─────────────┐    ┌─────────────┐    ┌─────────────┐
│    STATE    │ ━► │ PERFORMANCE │ ━► │   RESULTS   │
└─────────────┘    └─────────────┘    └─────────────┘
         ↕
┌─────────────┐
│ Physiology  │
└─────────────┘
```

Internal Representations

What and how you picture things inside your mind, plus what and how you say things to yourself, contribute towards the state you are in. How you perceive and represent the world to yourself powerfully affects your state. Your beliefs, values, attitudes and past experiences all affect the kinds of internal representations you make.

Physiology

In terms of our physiology, factors such as what we eat, drink, and how tired we are will all have an influence on our state. What is less well recognised is that other physiological factors can also affect your state positively or negatively. These include how you are breathing, your levels of muscular tension and your posture.

It is not always fully appreciated that the body and the mind are not two separate parts or divisions. They are one unified system. The body affects the mind and the mind affects the body.

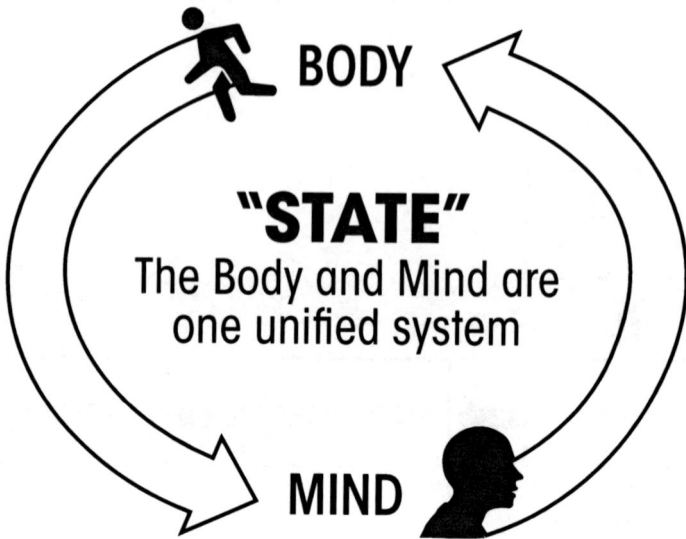

BODY

"STATE"
The Body and Mind are
one unified system

MIND

In order to demonstrate this, I would like to invite you to try an exercise I ask participants at my psychological training seminars to experience. Vividly imagine the following scene as it is described.

> 'Imagine that you are sitting at a table. On the table in front of you is a bowl of crushed ice. Sitting on top of the crushed ice is a very large and very juicy lemon that has been cut into quarters. Pick up one of the quarters of lemon. Notice how, when you squeeze it, drops of lemon juice ooze out of it. Lift up the quarter of lemon to your nose and smell the sharp scent of the lemon. Now place the quarter of lemon into your mouth and bite it, feeling the lemon juice burst all over your tongue!'

If you have imagined this scene vividly you will find that your mouth is now full of saliva. Merely biting the lemon in your imagination has resulted in a physical response from your body. What you have imagined in your mind has affected your body.

In a similar way, we will all have experienced our body affecting our mind. Feeling physically tired, for example, can affect how we are thinking and feeling. If we are experiencing any form of physical pain from an injury or illness, this may also affect how we are feeling mentally. Conversely, feeling well rested and healthy can help us to experience a more positive and happy state of mind.

Although we will all be able to identify with these influences, what is not always appreciated is that we can consciously use our physiology to change our state. It is literally possible to choose and change your state.

How to use your physiology to change your state

To demonstrate how physiology affects our state, imagine for a moment that you are feeling very negative and unhappy. Now move your body into the sort of posture it would be in if you felt like this. How would you sit or stand if you were feeling like this? Would you be slumped in your chair? How would your face look? Would you be frowning? How would your breathing be if you were feeling is this negative way? Would it be low and shallow? There will be a specific physiology that goes along with these negative thoughts.

Now let us change our state! Sit or stand in the posture you would be in if you were feeling very positive, confident and happy. How would you sitting or standing? Would you be upright with your shoulders back? How would your face look? Would you have a big smile on your face? How would you be breathing? Would it be deep and full? Again, there will be a specific physiology that goes along with these positive thoughts.

You will find it almost impossible to feel negative if you have a positive body posture. One way to change how you are feeling is to change your physiology. If you want to feel more positive, upbeat and confident sit, stand and move as if you are feeling positive, upbeat and confident. Because the body and mind are one unified system, your physiology will affect your mind and change the state you are in.

This powerful technique is deceptively simple. Please experiment with it and notice how you can change your state at will.

The power of setting anchors

I took my family to Disneyland Paris for a few days of fun. I really like roller coasters so I was delighted to discover that a brand new and very fast roller coaster had been introduced since the last time I was there.

The ride takes place inside a specially constructed building and is very fast, with steep ascents and drops, corkscrews, flashing lights and accompanying rock music.

At the start of the ride you get into your seat and are fastened in. Then a countdown starts with a loud voice: 'Five, four, three, two one!' After one it is almost like being shot out of a gun as you seem to go from nought to 60 in a second! In the space of a few seconds you go from horizontal to vertical at very high speed and your body reacts accordingly.

I enjoyed the ride so much that I went on it a second time! When I got into my seat a second time, even before the countdown had got to one, my body was already starting to react and feel like it was being affected by the G-force – even though we hadn't moved yet.

Without me realising it, the first time I had been on the ride my neurology (nervous system) had associated the experience of the countdown with the extreme experience of being accelerated forward at great speed.

The second time I experienced the countdown, my neurology went 'I know what happens now!' and started to generate the same physical responses as when I actually was shot forward at great speed.

Our minds naturally link experiences. Sometimes these associations are positive: for example, a favourite piece of music may bring back a pleasant memory. Each time that you hear the specific tune, it evokes the same pleasant feeling.

A stimulus which is linked to and triggers a physiological state is called an anchor. Anchors are usually external. When your alarm clock rings in the morning it is time to get up! A red traffic light means stop and a green traffic light means go.

The stimulus response concept

In each example above, something elicited a memory, feelings and behaviour.

Many years ago a Russian psychologist, Ivan Pavlov, conducted experiments into conditioned responses. As Pavlov studied dogs he discovered that they would salivate when they saw, smelt and tasted meat.

Pavlov added another stimulus to the meat. Whenever the dogs were being fed he rang a bell. After a few repetitions of ringing the bell as the dogs were fed, Pavlov discovered that he only had to ring the bell (without the presence of the meat) and the dogs would begin to salivate. The dogs had come to associate the ringing of the bell with the arrival of food and hence would salivate – without any food being present.

What do we mean by 'Anchoring'?

Anchoring is the process whereby a representation (this is frequently external) becomes linked to and triggers a response. Advertising makes use of anchors to produce a response every time a particular symbol, phrase or jingle is used.

How to establish useful Anchors

Now that we are aware of what anchors are and how they operate, we can use anchoring to get us into whatever mental state we desire at any time.

Using resourceful states (confidence, motivation, relaxation, calmness, focus) is one of the most effective ways to change your behaviour and therefore your performance.

Here are the steps for transferring positive resources from your past experiences to the present moment.

1. Take some time to get comfortable, either sitting or standing, then think of some specific situation where you would like to respond, behave and perform differently.

2. Next choose a specific state from the many different ones that you have experienced in the past that you would like to have available at any time. It could be any resourceful state – confidence, calmness, persistence, tenacity, resolve, determination, concentration etc.

3. When you have clarity about the resource you want available, recall a specific occasion when you experienced the specific resource. It is important that you choose the one that is the most clear and intense, so take your time.

4. If you cannot remember a time when you experienced the state you desire, then imagine somebody you know or know of who possesses the resource. You can even choose character from a film, television programme. What would it be like if you actually were this person experiencing the resourceful state? Although this may sound strange, especially if the person may not be real, please remember the feelings associated with the resourceful state are real and that is what important.

5. When you have a specific experience in mind, the next step is to choose the anchor that you will use to trigger the resourceful state you want whenever you want it.

The Kinaesthetic Element

Firstly we will establish the kinaesthetic (feeling/touch) element of your anchor. Touching your thumb and one of your fingers together works well as a kinaesthetic anchor.

Important considerations when choosing your kinaesthetic anchor are:

- It is unique, that is it is not something that you would do as part of your everyday behaviour. You want an anchor that is unique and distinctive so that it does not occur all the time. If this happened it could become associated with other states and lessen its effectiveness for you.

- You may also want your anchor to be something discrete if you need to be able to fire your anchor without being conspicuous.

The Auditory Element

Secondly, we will establish the auditory (sound/hearing) element of your anchor. This can be a word or phrase that you say to yourself either internally or aloud. It does not really matter what the word or phrase is, but ideally it should be in tune with the state that you wish to anchor. For example, using the word 'confident' for a confident state or 'power' for a powerful state would be appropriate.

The way that you say the word or phrase to yourself is as important as the word itself. The voice tone that you use is important. Ensure that it is distinctive and memorable. So, to build upon the words above, you would ensure that when you said 'confidence' you said it with a confident tone.

Another consideration when establishing an auditory anchor is to use music. You can choose to play any of your favourite tunes inside your head! Using the principle of anchoring it is possible to anchor your desired state to an appropriate piece of music.

The Visual Element

Thirdly we will establish the visual element of your anchor. You can choose any visual symbol.

One method is to imagine a circle of in colour of your choice and use that to establish your anchor. You can imagine the circle on the ground in front of you and step into it to establish your anchor.

Now that you have chosen an anchor in each representation system (kinaesthetic, auditory and visual), the next step is to recall and relive the state you desire to anchor.

1. Stand up. Take a step forward - it is very useful to have the state you wish to anchor in a different physical location – this helps to separate them cleanly.

2. In your imagination, recall the specific state that you have chosen to anchor. Remember what you were doing and imagine that you are back at that time, seeing what you were seeing. Now recall what sounds you were hearing. As you do this, start to re-experience the feelings that you felt. Take the time to relive the experience as fully as possible.

3. When the feelings peak and start to diminish, step back into the position you occupied before you stepped forward. You have now found out how best to re-experience and re-create the state you desire.

Putting it all together

Now you are ready to combine everything together and anchor the state you desire.

1. Once more, step forward into the same place as before and re-experience the state you wish to anchor again. Just before it reaches its peak, see the visual anchor, make your kinaesthetic gesture and say your word or phrase. The sequence of the three elements is not critical, use the order that you prefer.

2. It is very important to connect your anchors to the desired state as it is coming to its peak. The timing is very important. If you connect your anchors after the state has peaked, you would be anchoring the state decreasing, which is not what you want. Step out of the place where you are creating your anchors before the state has peaked.

3. Now to test the power of your anchor. Once you have stepped back take a few moments to change your state. Jump up and down and shake your arms and legs. This ensures you have broken the state you were in.

4. Now fire off your anchor again using all three elements (visual, auditory and kinaesthetic) and notice to what extent you access your desired state.

If you do not think the state is powerful enough, then go back and repeat the anchoring process again. You may need to repeat it a few times to ensure that the association between your anchor and your resourceful state is strong. Once you have established an effective anchor you will be able to use your anchors to summon the state you desire whenever you wish.

You may find that simply making your kinaesthetic gesture or 'firing your kinaesthetic anchor' is enough to summon the desired state, or you may wish to use all or some of the three anchors you have established. Experiment to find out what method works best for you.

You are, of course, not limited to establishing anchors for just one desired state. You can use the same process to anchor a range of desired states. I have a series of resourceful states, each anchored to different fingers and this gives me a very useful, almost 'push button' access to the states I choose.

Take the time to explore and experiment with this powerful technique and you will find that it makes a massive contribution to your performance.

How to talk to yourself

It's OK; there is no need to be alarmed! Talking to yourself, despite common misconceptions, is not a sign of mental illness. Talking to yourself, or 'Self Talk' as it is referred to by psychologists, is a powerful method of controlling your thinking, your state, and therefore your performance.

You are engaging in self-talk any time you carry on any form of dialogue with yourself. This could be giving yourself instructions and encouragement or interpreting what you are feeling about a situation. This dialogue can occur out loud or inside your head.

Self-talk has been defined as an "internal dialogue in which the individuals interpret feelings and perceptions, regulate and change evaluations and cognitions and give themselves instructions and reinforcement"[37]

Extensive research shows that positive self-talk has positive effects on performance.[38] [39] [40] [41]

The evidence of the power of self-talk on performance is most certainly not confined to the world of sport. Resrach by Ann Bernard from the University of New Orleans concluded that,

37   Hackfort, D., Scwenkmezger, P. (1993). Anxiety. In R.N. Singer, M. Murphy & L.K. Tennant (Eds.), *Handbook of research on sport psychology*, Macmillan
38   O'Connor, E.J., & Kirschenbaum, D.S. (1982). Something succeeds like success. Positive self monitoring for unskilled golfers. *Cognitive Therapy and Research*
39   Weinberg, R.S., Smith, J., Jackson,A., & Gould,D. (1984). Effect of association, dissociation and positive self-talk strategies on endurance performance. *Canadian Journal of Applied Sports Sciences*
40   Hamilton, S.A., & Fremour, W.J. (1985). Cognitive behavioural training for college basketball free throw performance. *Cognitive Therapy and Research*
41   Van Raalte, J.L., Brewer, B.W., Lewis, B.P., Linder, D.E., Wildman, G., & Kozimor, J. (1995) Cork! The positive effects of positive and negative self-talk an dart performance. *Journal of Sport Behaviour*

"Results indicated that there were significant differences between students who used more positive self-talk in the areas of academic and goal achievement; the data trends indicated the positive self-talk group did have higher levels of job performance. Overall, it was found that students with positive self-talk had higher levels of performance."[42]

Self-talk has been proven to be a powerful technique of cognitive control and as such can be an asset when it enhances feelings of self-worth and performance. However, it can equally be a dangerous liability when it is negative or if it becomes distracting to the task you are engaged in. In my experience, many people will say derogatory things about themselves or to themselves that they would never dream of saying to another person.

Cognitive-behavioural research shows that the ratio we have between positive coping thoughts and negative coping thoughts is important. One piece of research showed that "functional groups are characterized by a 1.7 to 1 ratio of positive to negative self-statements (positive dialogue), whereas mildly dysfunctional groups demonstrate a 1 to 1 ratio (internal dialogue of conflict)."[43]

This pattern of differences between positive self-talk and negative self-talk and its effect has been identified in a number of scenarios including research into levels of assertiveness[44], social anxiety[45], and self-esteem.[46]

The use of negative self-talk affects not just people's performance; it can affect people's overall self-esteem. In extreme cases this could lead to depression.

Certain forms of depression have been described as nothing more than a disorder of conscious thought and not a matter

42   Bernard, A., (2010) The effects of self-talk on the level of success of college students
43   Schwartz, R., M., (1986) The internal dialogue: On the asymmetry between positive and negative coping thoughts. *Cognitive Therapy and Research*
44   Schwartz, R.M., & Gottman, J.M. (1976). Toward a task analysis of assertive behaviour. *Journal of Consulting and Clinical Psychology*
45   Glass, C.R., & Merluzzi, T.V., (1981). Cognitive assessment of social evaluative anxiety. In T.V. Merluzzi, C.R. Glass, & M. Genest (Eds.) *Cognitive assessment*. Guildford Press
46   Vasta, R., & Brockner, J., (1979). Self-esteem and self-evaluative covert statements. *Journal of Consulting and Clinical Psychology*

of brain chemistry or anger turned inwards, as other theories maintain. Some depressed people simply think awful things about themselves and their future. Their symptom, negative self-talk, is their condition.

The raising of self-esteem through positive and effective self-talk will take time and patience. It is however, a process worth focusing upon.

Returning to our previous discussion of responsibility, it is worth focusing upon the powerful truth that self-esteem and confidence fundamentally begins and ends in our mind. Self-talk can play a powerful role in feeding positive and supportive suggestions into the mind. We are in charge of our minds and we can use them to support us to success.

Take charge of your mind

It can, of course, take effort to use positive self-talk to focus your mind on what you want to achieve, on your strengths and perhaps at times to ignore the comments and advice from others.

The effort involved will be rewarded by an improvement in self-esteem, confidence and performance. These factors begin and end in your own mind and self-talk is a powerful way of feeding the mind with 'positivity'.

Uses of Self-Talk

There are some specific areas in which you could choose to use self-talk:

Building Self-Efficacy

Earlier we explored the concept of self-efficacy. Self-efficacy was described as your perception of your confidence to succeed in a given task at a given time. It refers to specific/particular skills.

One of the ways that it is possible for self-efficacy to be enhanced is by 'verbal persuasion'. This refers to persuasive techniques used by you (or another person). You can therefore use self-talk as a method of enhancing self-efficacy, e.g. 'I can do this'.

Attention Control

Self-talk can also be used to help you to control and focus your attention. The ability to keep focused is a key skill for anyone to master.

Distractions of many kinds can disturb you during practice, performance or competition. Self-talk can be used to over-come any loss of attention with phrases such as 'keep focused', 'awareness' etc.

Mood Enhancement

Self-talk can be used to powerfully affect your mood. Self-talk can be used to regain a sense of calm and control if you become angry or tense ('mind like calm water', 'relax') and conversely be used to 'psych' yourself up if you are feeling bored, lethargic or tired ('come on!', 'let's do it!').

Improving Persistence and Effort

Self-talk is a very effective technique for helping to maintain effort, energy and persistence. We will all have times when we perhaps feel we are flagging somewhat. Self-talk can be very useful in such situations.

The use of 'go for it!', 'all the way!', 'push!' and so forth can be very motivating. I make extensive use of self-talk when I am running in marathons. I keep repeating positive phrases and/or words to myself and this helps to keep me running (albeit very slowly) all the way to the finish line.

What to say when you are talking to yourself

From the previous examples, you will have seen that it is important to keep your self-talk positive. It is worth stressing the three factors you need to keep in mind when considering the use of self-talk. Your self-talk should be:

- Positive
- Present Tense
- Personal

Positive

You must ensure you keep focused on what you do want to happen. A common mistake is to inadvertently focus on what don't want to happen.

The theory is that in order to make sense of a phrase your mind has to process it fully. Therefore, to make sense of 'Don't fall over', your mind has to process the concept of 'fall over'.

Some psychologists believe that the unconscious mind struggles to process negative commands and therefore you can be programming your unconscious mind with all sorts of things you don't want to happen e.g.

> 'Don't miss' – MISS
> 'Don't mess this up!' – MESS THIS UP
> 'Don't get angry' – GET ANGRY

A story related to me by a motivational speaker I was appearing with recently, concerned football manager Bobby Robson's 'motivational' pep talk to his team as they were about to take part in a penalty shoot out in a major international competition. According to the story, Robson marched up to his players and said: 'Right lads, there are thirty million people watching this at home, if you miss you will let them all down and you will remember it for the rest of your life'.

According to the theory discussed above, the unconscious minds of the players received the following input:

'Thirty million people watching, miss, let them down, remember it for the rest of your life.'

Therefore, ensure your self-talk is focused on what you do want to achieve, such as 'Win!' rather than 'Don't lose' and 'Focus' rather than 'Don't get distracted'.

Present tense

Keep your self-talk focused on the here and now. Focus on how you want to feel and perform at this moment. 'I am calm' is better than 'I will be calm'. This ensures that your self-talk has an immediate and positive effect.

Personal

Make your self-talk focused on… yourself! For example 'I can do this!'. Firstly you cannot do self-talk for anyone else or to affect anyone other than yourself. Secondly it is believed that the use of 'I' focuses the mind and enhances the effectiveness of the self-talk.

The power of Affirmations

One application of self-talk is the use of affirmations. Perhaps the most famous affirmation is that devised by French pharmacist Emile Coue in the 19th century: 'Every day, in every way, I am getting better and better'.

The theory behind affirmations is that the frequent and regular repetition of positive phrases programmes the suggestions into the unconscious mind which comes to accept them and act upon them as truths.

Many people attribute great power to the techniques of affirmation - I make extensive use of them myself. I would recommend you experimenting with writing some *positive + present tense + personal* affirmations and repeating them at least twice a day. The best times to do this are upon awakening and as you are falling off to sleep at night. At these times your brain wave activity is changing from the alpha state to the wide awake beta state in the morning and from beta to alpha state in the evening.

The unconscious mind is thought to be particularly receptive to suggestion when it is in the alpha state. Indeed this trance-like state is one of the states that hypnotists will utilise with their clients.

Examples of suitable affirmations would be:

'I am the national champion' (even before you are)

'Every day and in every way my (insert any skill) gets better and better.'

Please ensure you act upon what you have read, for it is only by applying the powerful performance-enhancement techniques you have learned so far that you will get the maximum benefit.

Create Your Future Now

The incredible power of imagery and mental rehearsal

Would you like to benefit from a mental training technique that is used almost universally by Olympic athletes? A major psychological study reported that more than 99% of Olympic athletes use imagery as part of their training programme.[47]

In addition, sports psychologists have identified that one of the characteristics of elite athletes is that they are more proficient at imagery than non-elite performers.

Before we look at what imagery is, let me first invite you to participate in an experiment that will demonstrate what it can do for you. Please only participate in this experiment if you are in good health.

- **Step 1**: Stand up, lift your right arm and point your index finger (if you are reading this book in a public place then you may choose to leave this experiment for later).

- **Step 2**: Keeping your feet pointing straight ahead, turn around clockwise as far as you can comfortably go. Take note of where your index finger is pointing on the wall behind you. Then return to the start position.

- **Step 3**: Put your right arm down by your side, close your eyes and in your mind imagine repeating the same movement. Imagine that as you do it, this time you find it much easier than the first time. Imagine when you reach the place where you stopped previously that you carry on turning around and notice that your finger is pointing to a place much further around than before.

- **Step 4**: Open your eyes, lift up your right arm and again point your index finger.

- **Step 5**: Keeping your feet pointing straight ahead, again turn around clockwise and this time notice how much further you actually turn around than the first time.

47   Orlick, T. and Partington, I., (1987) The sport psychology consultant: Analysis of critical components as viewed by Olympic athletes, *The Sport Psychologist*

When I ask participants at seminars to try this experiment, I usually hear gasps of astonishment as they discover how much further they turn around the second time.

Based upon the results of our simple experiment, and more importantly on the results of significant psychological research, it is clear that imagery can be very beneficial as a method of performance enhancement.

So what is imagery? Imagery can be defined as a 'symbolic sensory experience' that may occur in any sensory mode. It is sometimes referred to as 'visualisation', although this term implies that it only involves using the visual sensory mode. In fact imagery can, and indeed should, incorporate all sensory modes – visual (images), auditory (sound), kinaesthetic (touch/feeling), olfactory (smell) and gustatory (taste).

Imagery is a mental process or a mode of thought. Imagery uses all of the sensory modes to re-create or create an experience in the mind.

One of the most fascinating aspects of research into imagery is that when an individual engages in vivid imagery and absorbs themselves in it, their brain interprets the imagery as being identical to the actual situation itself. The brain appears to be unable to distinguish between a vividly imagined situation and a real situation.

Mental rehearsal, on the other hand, is defined as the employment of imagery to mentally practise an act. Thus mental rehearsal is a technique as opposed to merely a mental process. For example, you could imagine yourself working on and developing a skill that you want to improve. Although this sounds very simple, mental rehearsal is a very powerful method of performance enhancement.

Please be assured that using your imagination to rehearse is not some strange or mystical practice. It is a very common amongst all manner of athletes. Its use is not only confined to physical activity or sport. Mental rehearsal can be applied to any activity.

Having conducted an extensive review of the psychological research into mental rehearsal, I can report two robust conclusions:

Mental Rehearsal is better than no practice at all

Even if you do not manage to do any physical practice whatsoever at your chosen skill, mental rehearsal will help to improve your performance.

Mental Rehearsal combined with physical practice is more effective than either alone

Training physically and mentally, using physical practice and mental rehearsal, will improve your performance more than physical training on its own.

So how can you apply these powerful conclusions? I am certainly not advocating that you abandon physical skill training, but there may be times when it may not be possible for you to train physically.

For example, with sport you may be recovering from an injury or an illness that prevents you from training physically. Or personal circumstances may prevent you from being able to attend training on a particular day. On occasions such as these, you can still gain the benefit of practising mentally. You can mentally rehearse what you would have done physically.

There is a famous story about an American army officer who was held captive for several years during the Vietnam War. In order to keep himself occupied he would play a game of golf in his imagination every day. When he was finally released from captivity, he went to play an actual game of golf for the first time in many years. He played one of the best games of golf in his life - the many years of mental rehearsal had resulted in a huge improvement in his physical golfing performance.

However, the real power of mental rehearsal is when it is combined with physical practice. As detailed above, psychological research confirms that mental rehearsal combined with physical practice is more effective than either alone.

The individual who practises physically and rehearses mentally will have a distinct advantage over the individual who only practises physically.

Almost 100% of Olympic athletes surveyed by sports psychologists reported the use of mental rehearsal. Elite athletes use this technique for one reason and one reason only – it works. Mental rehearsal is a powerful performance enhancement method.

If you really want to release your full potential, then you must add mental rehearsal to your training and preparation schedule.

Why is Mental Rehearsal so powerful?

A considerable amount of scientific research has been done into mental rehearsal and how powerful it can be in improving performance.

According to Dr. Charles Garfield, president of the Performance Sciences Institute, the Russians have extensively researched and applied the relationship between imagery or mental rehearsal and performance.

In one study,[48] a group of elite Russian athletes were divided into four groups:

- Group One spent 100% of their time engaging in physical training.
- Group Two spent 75% of their time engaging in physical training and 25% of their time mentally rehearsing the exact movements and accomplishments they wanted to achieve in their sport.
- Group Three spent 50% of their time engaging in physical training and 50% of their time mentally rehearsing.
- Group Four spent 25% of their time engaging in physical training and 75% of their time mentally rehearsing.

At the 1980 Winter Olympic Games in Lake Placid, New York, the fourth group showed the greatest improvement in performance followed by groups three, two and one in that order.

An Australian psychologist, Alan Richardson, has obtained similar results with basketball players. He took three groups of basketball players and tested their ability to make free throws.

---

48   Garfield, C., (1985) *Peak Performance: Mental Training Techniques of the World's Greatest Athletes* Warner Books

- Group One were instructed to spend 20 minutes a day practising free throws.
- Group Two were instructed not to practise free throws.
- Group Three were instructed to spend 20 minutes a day mentally rehearsing shooting perfect baskets.

Group Two, who did no practice, showed no improvement. Group One improved by 24% and Group Three, who had only rehearsed or practised mentally, improved by an astonishing 23% - almost as much as the group who had engaged in physical practice.[49]

These examples are just two out of hundreds of psychological experiments that clearly demonstrate the power of mental rehearsal.

How does Mental Rehearsal work?

Two of the main theories concerning mental rehearsal are the 'muscle memory' (or psychoneuromuscular) theory and the 'mental blueprint' (or symbolic learning) theory.

Muscle Memory Theory

Psychologists hypothesise that mental rehearsal works because muscles become innervated (stimulated) sufficiently during mental rehearsal to give kinaesthetic (body sensation) feedback to the body parts that will be involved in the actual physical practise. The theory is that during mental rehearsal your muscles 'learn' just as they do when you are actually performing the movement.

Mental Blueprint Theory

A further theory of how mental rehearsal works is symbolic learning theory. This hypothesises that the imagery used in mental rehearsal may function as a coding system that helps individuals to acquire or understand behaviour patterns.

The mental rehearsal may help you to blueprint or code your behaviour into symbolic components, thus making the movement more familiar and perhaps more automatic.

49   Richardson, A., (1967) Mental Practice: A review and discussion. *Research Quarterly*

Whatever theory or theories are correct about why mental rehearsal works, one fact remains certain – it works! So let us now look at some ways that you can apply mental rehearsal.

Mental rehearsal can be used to get the very best out of yourself. You will make faster progress to achieving your goals if you use mental rehearsal.

Some of the ways that you can use mental rehearsal:

- To practise new sporting moves or techniques before performing them physically. It can be useful to break down complicated sequences into manageable sections and then build this up to the full sequence.

- To practise moves or techniques that you already practise physically. The process of mental rehearsal will powerfully complement and enhance your physical practice.

- Immediately before important events. This can strengthen confidence by calling up the feelings you have associated with a good performance. Mental rehearsal will also focus your attention on the task at hand.

- If you have limited physical practice time available before a specific event.

- If you are recovering from injury – you can still get some beneficial sports training completed, even though you may be unable to train physically.

How to make your mental rehearsal more powerful

When people first begin to practise mental rehearsal, they can find themselves getting distracted or feeling restless. It is therefore recommended that, to begin with, you carry out your mental rehearsal in a state of deep relaxation.

Relaxing in this way will support you as you practise mentally rehearsing. Mental rehearsal is a skill, and like any other skill, it requires practise in order to become proficient at it.

So, when beginning your practice of mental rehearsal, try to sit or lie down somewhere comfortable. If at all possible, reduce any distractions such as interruptions from other people and noise from sources such as the television, telephone etc.

If there is unavoidable background noise then you may wish to mask this using soft classical or 'new age' style music played at a low volume. As you become more proficient at mental rehearsal, such considerations will not be required. You will quite quickly be able to mentally rehearse in almost any environment – on a bus, on the tube, queuing in shops and sitting, standing or lying down.

When you are sitting or lying comfortably, begin to focus all your attention on your breathing. Focus on how the air feels as it goes in and out of your nose. Concentrate fully upon this. Gradually make your breathing deeper and fuller. As you do this, shift your concentration from how the air feels going in and out of your nose and begin to experience how it feels as it goes in and out of your lungs. Continue to focus upon making your breathing fuller and deeper. Several minutes of concentration upon your breathing should produce a sufficiently relaxed state for mental rehearsal.

It is recommended that you regularly set aside some time every day to practise mental rehearsal. Five to 15 minutes per day will be sufficient. As you become more proficient, you can practise mental rehearsal at any convenient moment during the day. To begin your practice of mental rehearsal, imagine the place where you would normally perform the skill you wish to improve. With a sporting example this could be a sports ground, or for a business example the conference hall where you are to deliver a speech to an audience of thousands.

Imagine how it looks, smells, sounds and feels

An important element that can enhance your mental rehearsal is to re-emphasise that although sometimes referred to as 'visualisation', mental rehearsal does not involve only the visual mode. It can, and indeed should, incorporate all sensory modes – visual (seeing), auditory (sounds), kinaesthetic (feelings), olfactory (smells) and gustatory (tastes).

In this way, when you are mentally rehearsing, you are creating a rich sensory experience. The more vivid and accurate you can make this experience, the greater your chances of replicating this in the real life situation.

When you have successfully imagined the environment in which you will be using the skill(s) you wish to improve, imagine yourself performing the skill(s). Imagine playing the sport, imagine making the speech.

You can imagine yourself from either an internal perspective (seeing with your own eyes) or from an external perspective (seeing from the perspective of watching yourself as if you were being filmed by a video camera or watched by another person).

Research has shown that elite athletes are more likely to mentally rehearse from an internal perspective than non-elite athletes. Internal imagery has been shown to produce more neuromuscular activity than external imagery. It is therefore recommended that you experiment and mentally rehearse with both perspectives.

As you become more proficient at creating and controlling appropriate images, gradually increase the complexity of the actions that you are mentally rehearsing.

Practising mental rehearsal can be tiring, especially in the beginning. Short-term periods of quality imagery are better than longer-term periods of low quality imagery.

Regular and committed practice will deliver the dual benefit of performance enhancement and more disciplined control of your mind. This will bring you significant benefits in many areas of your life.

Mental rehearsal is one of the fundamental skills of mental training and the benefits that it brings can be significant. As the speaker and writer Jim Rohn has said, 'Success is neither magical nor mysterious. Success is the natural consequence of consistently applying basic fundamentals.'

The power of sub-modalities

The same senses that we use to experience the outside world (sight, sound, taste, smell, touch) are also used to store and represent ('re-present') experiences in our mind.

If I ask you to remember what colour your front door is, you will probably make a mental picture (an internal representation) of it in order to do so. You use internal representations to think.

The combination of pictures, voices, sounds, tastes and smells that you remember from the past, or imagine in the future affect how you are thinking and feeling. They will affect your state.

Your state, thoughts and beliefs can be changed by experimenting with what are known as 'sub-modalities'.

If the various senses (sight, hearing, touch, smell and taste) are modalities – ways of experiencing the world – then sub-modalities can be described as 'the building blocks of the senses'. They are the components that make up each modality. They enable our brains to sort and code our experiences. As you begin to notice your thoughts, you will be able to notice the modalities and then the varying sub-modalities.

Sub-modalities can be thought of as being the most fundamental operating code of the human brain. You cannot think any thought or recall any memory without it having a sub-modality structure. Putting your awareness onto the sub-modality structure of your experiences can prove very interesting.

Sub-modality distinctions

What follows are three lists that contain examples of some sub-modality differences or distinctions. As you become aware of these, you will find that you become increasingly conscious of the various sub-modalities that form part of your thinking processes (for simplicity Olfactory and Gustatory have been left out of this list).

Visual (Seeing)	
Black and White – Colour	Framed – Panoramic
Near – Far	Moving – Still
Bright – Dim	Three Dimensional – Flat
Size	Angle viewed from
Focused – Defocused	Distance

Auditory (Hearing)	
Location	High Pitch – Low Pitch
Direction	Tonality
Internal – External	Timbre
Loud – Soft	Pauses
Fast – Slow	Duration

Kinaesthetic (Feeling)	
Location	Duration
Size	Vibration
Shape	Pressure
Intensity	Heat
Steady	Weight
Movement	

For many people the most interesting aspect of sub-modalities is what happens when you change them. Some can be changed and make little difference. Others can be far more impactful.

Experimenting with Sub-Modalities

As an experiment, sit down somewhere comfortable. Take a few deep breaths and turn your attention inwards. Think of a situation in your past that has emotional significance for you.

To begin, become aware of the visual part of the memory. Imagine bringing the image closer, then push it far away. What difference does this make and which do you prefer? Before you move on, put it back as it was originally.

Then imagine yourself turning up and down a brightness control just as you would on a television set. Notice what difference it makes when you do this. Again before you move on put the brightness back to where it was originally.

Next, bring your attention to the colour of the image. Is the image in colour or is it black and white or perhaps somewhere in between? First, make the image full colour and notice what happens. Then drain all colour out of the image, turn it black and white and again notice what happens.

Carry on your experiment with other visual sub-modalities and then do the same with the auditory (e.g. louder/softer) and kinaesthetic (e.g. high pressure/low pressure) sub-modalities.

Some or all of these changes will have a profound impact on how you feel about the memory. By experimenting with sub-modalities you can discover powerful ways to alter, for instance, your motivation.

For example, if I wish to motivate myself about something I need to do, I make an internal picture of the thing I want to do, make it full colour and bring the picture closer. This has the effect of motivating me to want to do it.

As a further experiment, think of something that you really want to do. Choose something you really enjoy and are highly motivated to complete.

Notice the sub-modality structure. What are the various visual, auditory and kinaesthetic elements?

Next, think of something you most definitely don't want to do. It might be something you need to get done but you don't want to do it.

Notice the sub-modality structure. What are the various visual, auditory and kinaesthetic elements?

What are the distinctions or the differences between the thing you really want to do and the thing you really don't want to do? What are the differences in the visual, auditory and kinaesthetic sub-modalities?

As an experiment, apply the sub-modality distinctions from the thing you really want to do to the thing you really don't want to do, and notice what happens.

How differently do you feel about doing the thing you previously didn't want to do? Perhaps you feel more motivated to do it. If so, then you have discovered a very simple way to enhance your motivation.

Using Sub-Modalities to change beliefs

A similar process can be used to alter beliefs that don't empower you. For example, select something you don't currently believe that you can do.

- Once again, notice the sub-modality structure. What are the various visual, auditory and kinaesthetic elements?
- Now think of something you are absolutely certain that you can do, such as walking, riding a bike, reading this book etc.
- Notice the sub-modality structure. What are the various visual, auditory and kinaesthetic elements?
- Finally, apply the sub-modality structure of the thing you are absolutely certain you know how to do to the thing you don't currently believe you can do and... notice what has changed.

Perhaps you will have succeeded in very swiftly and easily changing a belief that has been limiting you or holding you back. Welcome to your new exciting future!

Using Sub-Modalities to change past memories

If I wish to diminish the effect of an unpleasant memory, I make the picture of it black and white and then make the picture very small and far away. This neutralises the effect the memory has.

Experiment for yourself and discover what happens. You may choose to leave the memory with the sub-modalities at the values you like best.

Perceptual Positions

Have you ever taken a ride on a roller coaster? As you remember a time when you had an experience like this, you may remember the feelings of speed, exhilaration or even fear.

Now, if you remember a time when you watched other people taking a ride on a roller coaster you will notice that things are different. Usually there is a marked difference between recalling the feelings of actually doing something and recalling the feelings of watching someone else doing it.

One of the many interesting areas to explore about the structure of how we think is in the area of what is known as 'perceptual positions'. I invited you to remember being on a roller coaster. As you did this you probably imagined the event as though you were looking through your own eyes.

This is known as 'first position'. It is the perspective of looking out of your own eyes.

You can also choose to imagine an event, be it in the future or the past, from the other person's perspective. This is known as 'second position'. This is as if you are looking at someone else through their eyes.

You can further enhance you experience by imagining the event from the perspective of an observer, someone who is watching the interaction but is not involved. This is known as 'third position'.

Using these three perceptual positions can be very useful. We can use first position to remember successes from the past and how good we felt about them and use this to manage our state – how we are thinking and feeling.

We can use second position to imagine how a person we will interact with may perceive us. Many people report quite startling insights into themselves and their abilities when they imagine looking at themselves from another's perspective. It can provide a fresh insight and way of thinking about things that can be very powerful.

We can use third position to get a more detached point of view. It is as though you are an independent observer with no personal involvement in the situation. This perceptual position can be very useful to recall and review your performance in a particular event and situation from a more objective viewpoint, rather than have it clouded with the emotion that may accompany perceiving it from first or second position.

We all spend time in these three positions naturally, and they help us to understand and get a fuller perspective on things. The ability to consciously move between them can provide richness and greater choice.

Get Focused

How to develop rock solid concentration

The ability to concentrate and focus is vitally important to your success. Concentration is the ability to focus your attention on whatever is important without being distracted by irrelevant things.

Once you have developed and strengthened your ability to concentrate intensely, you find that all irrelevant stimuli will seem to fade into the background. As a result your performance will improve.

In our complex, modern world it may seem as if we are constantly bombarded with sensory information. We experience on an ongoing basis what can at times seem like a flood of information – what we see, what we hear, what we feel, what we smell and what we taste.

Today, advertisers, political parties, charities and businesses all attempt to attract our attention. Although it may at times seem as if you are sensing many things at once, in reality your brain is scanning the environment and jumping from one area of attentional focus to another.

Developing rock solid concentration requires motivation and self-discipline. You will be required to make a conscious effort to pay attention to important things. One thing is certain – by concentrating on your concentration it will improve. The ability to mentally focus is a key trait in achieving a state of optimum mental preparation and performance.

You need to develop the ability to adapt your focus to suit the demands of differing situations. For example, you may wish to have a wide field of focus in a team meeting where it is useful to keep an awareness of the total picture. Whereas when writing a report at your computer, you may need to keep fewer elements in your awareness.

It may take time and effort to develop a laser-like focus but the rewards are great. If a steeplejack was using explosives to demolish a chimney next door to where you were, you would shift your attention just long enough to assess the situation, decide it wasn't important and then refocus, ready to continue as if nothing had distracted you.

Narrow and broad focus

It is important to be aware of how you focus, how you pay attention. It can be useful to think of your focus as a searchlight. You can turn it where you choose.

You can use it to light up a wide area or narrow the beam down to focus on a particular target. You can have a broad focus or a narrow focus.

To experience a broad focus, let your attention go wide. Look around the room you are in at the moment. See as much as you possibly can, without being drawn to specific details. How much is it possible for you to experience?

To experience narrow focus, choose an object in the room and look closely at it. What can you see? Pick out the details. The more of the detail you see, the less overall you can see.

Internal and external focus

Now that you have experienced the differences between a narrow and broad focus we can look at what you are paying attention to.

There two possibilities. You can be focused externally, concentrating outwards or focused internally, concentrating inwards.

In the previous exercise you experienced a broad and narrow focus externally. Now let us do the same thing internally.

To experience a broad internal focus; gradually become aware of your whole body so that you experience full body awareness. To experience narrow internal focus, narrow your attention down to once specific area of your body – your right hand, for example. How does that feel? How different is it to the previous experience?

We now have four categories of attention:

- Narrow External
- Broad External
- Narrow Internal
- Broad Internal

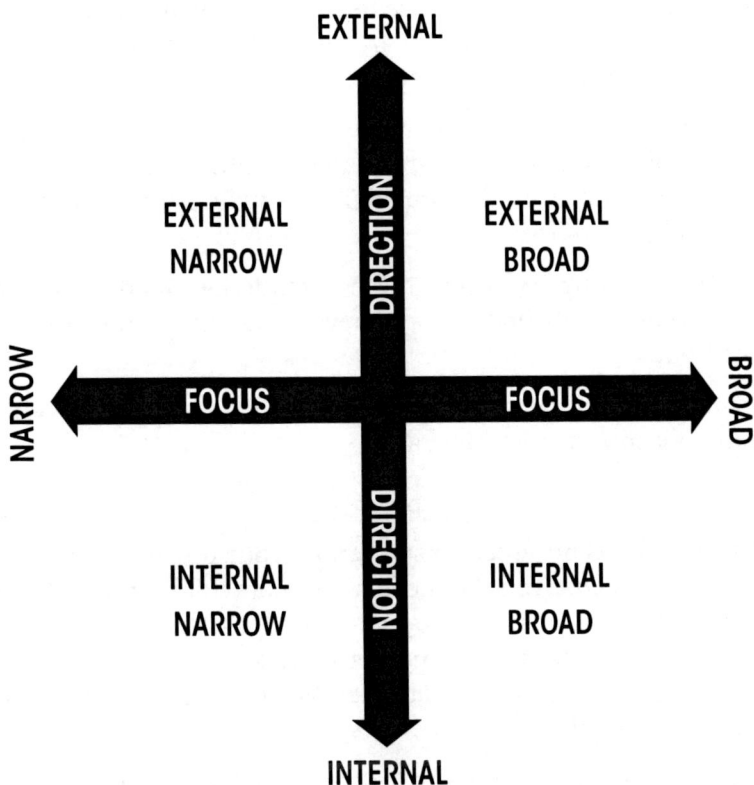

EXTERNAL

EXTERNAL NARROW	**DIRECTION**	**EXTERNAL BROAD**

NARROW ← **FOCUS** | **FOCUS** → **BROAD**

INTERNAL NARROW	**DIRECTION**	**INTERNAL BROAD**

INTERNAL

The top left hand quadrant is a narrow external attention focus. This is used when you require a strong intense focus upon one thing. A broader focus in this circumstance could prove too distracting.

The top right hand quadrant is a broad external attention focus. This is used when you want to maintain awareness. I use this type of focus when running seminars as it allows me to remain aware of everyone in the audience and how they are responding. Too narrow a focus in these circumstances and I would not be paying sufficient attention to all the people in the room.

The bottom left hand quadrant is a narrow internal attention focus. An example of an appropriate use of this type of attention would be when you go inside and mentally rehearse.

The bottom right hand quadrant is a broad internal focus. An example of an appropriate use for this type of attention would be to check how balanced you are feeling from an overall physical, mental and emotional perspective.

No one quadrant is better or worse than any other. Getting a balance and using them appropriately is what is important. Do not allow yourself to get 'stuck' in one style, perhaps through personal preference.

Practise moving between these attentional quadrants and developing the flexibility to alter your attention and focus as required.

Let us now look at some specific ways that you can develop your concentration and focus.

EXERCISE ONE

This exercise is designed to strengthen your powers of concentration and focus. You will need a piece of white card, or if this is not available some white paper will do. On the piece of card/paper use a felt tip pen or marker to make a circle of approximately two centimetres in diameter. Make the circle as neat and round as possible.

You will also need some form of stop watch or method of timing the exercise and a pen/pencil and paper.

The exercise is deceptively simple. Place the piece of card/paper in an upright position on a table in front of you and sit where you can look at it comfortably.

The object of the exercise is to focus all your attention upon the circle to the exclusion of everything else. Although this sounds a very simple task, you will probably find it very challenging to begin with to maintain concentration/focus upon the circle for any length of time.

As soon as you realise your attention has wandered, make a note of how long you were able to maintain concentration/focus.

This simple exercise, if practised diligently will strengthen your powers of concentration and focus. As you progress with practising on a regular basis, the length of time you can maintain concentration and focus will increase.

It is important to keep a record of your times as this will prove that you are making progress.

EXERCISE TWO

This exercise is designed to develop your ability to firstly switch your attention, and secondly to screen out distractions.

To practise this exercise you will need to have two sources of sound. For example, you could use your television and a radio or other music / sound source.

Switch on your two sound sources and if at all possible have spoken voices, rather than music, coming from both of them. Ensure that both sound sources are set at the same volume.

Sit or stand between the sound sources. In order to explain the exercise we will describe the sound sources as 'Sound source A' and 'Sound source B'.

To begin the exercise, do not focus on one sound source in particular. After a few moments, focus your attention on sound source A and attempt to block out sound source B.

After you have done this for a minute or so switch your focus onto the sound source B and attempt to block out sound source A. Then keep repeating the exercise, switching the focus of your attention every minute or so.

With practice your ability to switch focus and to screen out distractions will improve significantly.

EXERCISE THREE

This exercise will enhance your ability to shift the focus of your awareness through the four quadrants above. It is easier to do this exercise sitting down.

To begin, focus your attention on one specific area in the room you are in. Fully focus your attention on one specific spot. Study the spot intently and concentrate fully upon it.

After a few minutes of this, allow your awareness to expand and take in more and more of the room you are in. What can you see out of the corner of your eyes? Allow your awareness to expand as fully as possible. If you could see behind you without turning your head around, what would you see? Although we cannot actually do this, the act of thinking about it can help to broaden our awareness.

After a few minutes of this broad awareness, become aware of your breathing. Begin to focus your attention upon your breathing. Keep your eyes open and focus more and more upon your breathing. How does the air feel as it goes in and out of your nose? Notice how the air feels as it goes in and out of your lungs.

After a few minutes, expand your awareness out to feel all your body. How does your whole body feel? How balanced are you feeling?

You can experiment with this exercise by altering the order of the four elements of the exercise. This will develop your ability to control the focus of your attention at will which will allow you to switch your attention as appropriate for the situation at hand.

I wish you the greatest success in developing your ability to concentrate. The quest to develop rock-solid concentration and laser-like focus can be challenging. It will, however, deliver great rewards to you.

Chill Out

How to relax and control stress

Whilst it is true that stress, tension, failure, setbacks and pain are perhaps unpleasant things to contemplate, their existence is a reality. Indeed, a person who is committed to winning and to being successful is likely to encounter challenge, effort, failure, setbacks, pain and tension on the journey to significant achievement.

Therefore, it makes sense that you learn not only how to cope with such demands but to thrive upon them.

Successful people will focus their attention on the work they need to do to get where they want to go. However, this needs to be balanced with adequate rest, recovery and relaxation.

Dealing with stress

A successful person will need to juggle the various demands and challenges that they have chosen and also to ensure they place sufficient focus on the key areas of their life. If you want to get more you have to do more. This could be thought of as being potentially 'stressful'.

Stress is a natural response to any real or potential threats in our environment. It is a result of our inbuilt, primitive fight or flight survival instinct.

Stress is conjured up by our perceptions of what is 'out there' in the world. The good news is that as 'stress' is inside us we have the ability to take responsibility for and deal with it effectively.

A leading expert in the area of stress, Dr Hans Selye categorises stress into two forms:

- Eustress: this is stress that is pleasant and desirable.
- Distress: this is stress that is harmful and unpleasant.

Selye further defines stress as: 'The non-specific response of the body to any demand; whether it is caused by, or results in, pleasant or unpleasant conditions.' [50]

It is possible to change your perception of stress from something that is negative to something that is positive.

For example, without 'stress' you might find that you lose your competitive edge. Many successful sports people report that they actually thrive on the pressure, excitement or stress of competition. These things give an extra 'edge' to their performance.

In the course of my work I regularly give speeches to large audiences of people, sometimes over a thousand people at a time. I do not see this as stressful; I find it exciting and positive.

Our perception of any event will be different from someone else's. I am aware that for some people the thought of standing on a stage and giving a talk to a thousand people would be their worst nightmare, yet for me it is something pleasurable.

The choice about how you think about any situation in your life will always be yours.

The world will not change because we do not like some aspect of it. There are some things that you will be able to influence and some that you will not. Perhaps one way of thinking about stress is to fully realise this.

There is a Buddhist concept known as 'What is, is'. When you adopt this attitude you can stop wasting mental, emotional and physical energy on attempting to change things that cannot be changed.

This does not mean that you passively accept everything that happens in life. Where you can and want to make a change, make it. However, it is important to recognise the things that you can do nothing about and to stop wasting your time and energy complaining and worrying about them.

Or as professional speaker Larry Wingett puts it: 'Shut Up, Stop Whining and Get A Life!'

---

50   Selye, H., (1974) *Stress without distress*, Lippincott Williams & Wilkins

The well known 'Serenity Prayer' says:

> *'God grant me the serenity to accept the things I cannot change, the courage to change the things I can, and the wisdom to know the difference.'*

The well known spiritual book, *A Course in Miracles*, contains the powerful concept of 'I could choose peace instead of this'.

Whatever your personal views, be they religious, spiritual, atheist or agnostic, there is wisdom in the above concepts. If you allow the external world to control your internal state then you be at the mercy of events that occur. By choosing to take responsibility for yourself and your thoughts and feelings you will be in charge - whatever happens.

How to remain calm and composed

Earlier we looked at the concept of state management as a way of controlling our thoughts and feelings. We explored the two main components that affect and (are affected by) our state:

- Internal representations
- Physiology

Internal representations

What and how do you picture things inside your mind, plus what and how you say things to yourself, contribute towards the state you are in. How you perceive and represent the world to yourself powerfully affects your state. Your beliefs, values, attitudes and past experiences all affect the kinds of internal representations you make.

Physiology

Factors such as what we have eaten, drunk, and how tired we are will all have an influence on our state. What is less well recognised is other physiological factors can also affect your state positively or negatively. These include how you are breathing, your levels of muscular tension and your posture.

We also explored the body-mind system and the concept that the body and the mind are not two separate parts or divisions.

They are one unified system. The body affects the mind and the mind affects the body.

With these concepts in mind let us now look at some specific things we can do to remain calm and composed.

Becoming agitated or too excited (what sports psychologists refer to as over-arousal) can cause a general increase in muscular tension, a narrowing of the visual field and make you easier to distract. This state would clearly not be conducive to exceptional performance.

So here are a number of things you can do to remain calm or composed. These same techniques can be used to regain a calm and composed state if you find yourself feeling agitated, stressed or over-excited.

Breathing techniques

A powerful way to affect how you are feeling is to utilise breathing techniques. The specific breathing technique called 'Ha Breathing' that was discussed earlier increases personal energy, calmness and confidence.

To briefly recap, the process of Ha Breathing makes the out breath twice as long as the in breath. You take twice as long to breathe out as you to do breathe in.

When practising Ha Breathing, breathe from the diaphragm. This is at the bottom of your rib cage. With diaphragmatic breathing, your stomach goes in and out – which is one way to check you are breathing from the correct place.

This is how you do Ha Breathing:

- Sit or stand comfortably, in a balanced posture with your feet flat on the floor.

- Breathe in deeply through your nose. When you breathe in your stomach should come out. If you put your hand on your stomach you will be able to feel when you are doing this correctly. As you breathe in, your lungs fill with air, your diaphragm moves down, and your stomach comes out.

- Exhale out through the mouth making a long 'Haaaaaaaa aaaaaaaaaaaaaaaaaaaaaa' sound. The out breath should be twice as long as the in breath.

Ha breathing is an excellent breathing technique for gaining or maintaining a calm and composed state.

Other useful breathing techniques are to breathe slowly and deeply as in Ha Breathing and to add the power of your imagination. As you breathe in say the word 'in' to yourself and imagine energy flowing into your body. As you breathe out say the word 'out' to yourself and imagine any stress and tension leaving your body.

Centring Yourself

Centring is a useful technique that you can use to become calm and composed. It is easy to do and after some practise you will become proficient very quickly. This can be done either standing or sitting down and the process is:

- Close your eyes and breathe deeply.
- For a moment hold your breath while feeling a few of your heartbeats.
- Exhale and repeat until you feel calm.
- Now breathe normally and imagine energy radiating from the centre of your body, and then expanding to fill your entire body.
- Feel your feet connect to the earth.
- Allow your mind to clear and your body to relax with every breath.
- Open your eyes and continue with whatever you wish to do.

With continued practice you will discover that you are able to remain centred for longer and longer periods of time.

This is a deceptively simple mental trick, which almost seems too ridiculous to be as effective as it is.

All you need to do to benefit from this technique is that whenever you wish to feel calm and composed, imagine that you are inside a giant clear glass bubble that surrounds your entire body.

Nothing that is negative or stressful in any way can get through the protective surface of your bubble. From the calm environment of your giant bubble you can survey the outside world from a different perspective.

Whilst I appreciate that this idea may seem somewhat strange, it is utilised by many top sportspeople. It is believed that the brain cannot distinguish between something that is real and something that is vividly imagined and it is this fact that makes this technique so effective.

It can be used in all sorts of different situations and provides a calm and still place where you can regain or retain a peaceful state of mind at any time.

How to use meditation

Some people make the mistake of confusing the practical skill of meditation with some form of bizarre, mystical practice.

Meditation is a natural faculty of the human mind. Although it has and is linked to some religious and spiritual practices, it is a practical skill in its own right.

The regular practice of meditation will help you to reach a deep state of relaxation, greater peace of mind and it facilitates concentration by disciplining the mind. All of these factors will make a positive contribution to your performance.

Four basic components are common to most types of meditation:

1.   A quiet environment
2.   A comfortable position
3.   A mental device
4.   A passive attitude

A mental device can be a mantra or an object that can be used as a focus of awareness and/or contemplation. This helps to switch the mind from logical, externally orientated thought by providing a focus of attention on something that is non-arousing and non-stimulating.

A mantra is often a non-stimulating meaningless rhythmic sound of one or two syllables that a person repeats regularly whilst meditating. Alternatively it can be a single word or longer affirmation.

To meditate, get into a comfortable position, in a quiet environment where you will not be disturbed. You can meditate when walking, standing up, lying or sitting down. However, most meditators favour a sitting position. You do not have to sit in the lotus position!

Sitting in the right posture will help your meditation. It is important to sit with a straight back. This helps you to breathe properly and has the effect of helping you to feel alert and awake.

When sitting, relax your shoulders, rest your hands in your lap or on your thighs but do not cross your arms. Your head needs to face forward – neither up nor down.

Your eyes can be closed or, if you are feeling drowsy, open but lowered and unfocused.

You can use a straight-backed chair or sit on one or more firm cushions on the floor.

Here are two meditation variations for you to experiment with:

Breath meditation

During the practice you will be focusing on the in and out flow of your breath.

You can do this by focusing on one of three places. Choose whichever you prefer:

1. The tip of your nose, the point where the breath enters your body.
2. Your chest, feeling it rise and fall.
3. Your lower stomach, about two centimetres below your belly button.

To begin, get comfortable and start to clear your mind. Relax the body and focus your attention on your breathing.

As you breathe in and out, count your breaths up to five or 10 repeatedly. This helps to anchor your mind to your breathing.

You can choose to either count on each out breath only (e.g.('one... two... three...') or double count on the in breath and the out breath ('one, one... two, two... three, three...').

If you lose the count or the breath, just return to it without becoming annoyed with yourself.

Practise for as long as you like. You may find that five to 10 minutes is sufficient to begin with, and with regular practise 20 to 30 minutes will become possible.

Mantra Meditation

During this meditation, you will be focusing your attention on a mantra. This is a sound, single word or phrase you will be repeating throughout the meditation.

To begin, choose your mantra. 'Om' or 'Ohm' is a famous example. Other people use mantras that consist of meaningless syllables.

Other options include the use of a word such as 'one', 'relax', 'peace' or affirmations such as 'slow down', 'relax', 'let go', 'easy' etc.

Start by getting comfortable and clearing your mind. Take a few deep breaths and relax. Repeat your mantra either silently or out loud. Use the same mantra throughout your meditation.

The mantra is repeated with full attention on the sound or on the rhythm of the breath. The mantra acts as an anchor that helps the mind to quieten and become focused.

If you find yourself becoming distracted, or your attention drifts, just bring your attention back to your mantra and continue. Again, practise for as long as you choose.

When practised regularly, meditation can bring many benefits including relaxation, focus, a calm attitude and an increase in Alpha brainwave activity.

A simple trick with your eyes that can eliminate stress in seconds

This is a powerful technique that utilises the mind-body connection. As previously discussed, the mind and the body are not two separate or distinct things. They are elements of one unified system.

Therefore, the mind influences the body and the body influences the mind. We can use this fact to virtually eliminate stress in a matter of seconds.

The autonomic nervous system controls your involuntary actions (heartbeat, breathing, digestion etc). It has two divisions:

- **The sympathetic nervous system** prepares the body for stressful or demanding situations.

- **The parasympathetic nervous system** operates in quiet, non-stressful situations.

These two aspects of your nervous system exhibit different physical characteristics, as follows:

Sympathetic	Parasympathetic
• Ciliary (focus) muscle in the eye relaxes, the lens flattens and thins	• Ciliary (focus) muscle in the eye contracts, lens is more rounded.
• Focus on distant objects	• Focus on nearby objects
• Heart rate increases	• Heart rate decreases
• Adrenal glands produce stress hormones	
• Blood vessels in lungs constrict slightly	
• Stomach decreases production of digestive enzyme	• Stomach secretes more digestive enzyme and acid
• Intestinal movement of food slows down	• Intestinal movement of food speeds up
• Bladder sphincter muscle contracts	• Bladder sphincter muscle relaxes
• Skin blood vessels constrict	
• Sweat pores open	
• Saliva is thick and viscous	• Saliva is thin and copious

This stress-reducing technique utilises the fact that:

- Eyes mainly in fovial (forward/looking straight ahead) vision are linked to the sympathetic nervous system.
- Eyes mainly in peripheral (sideways looking) vision are linked to the parasympathetic nervous system.

The key application of these facts is that when you put more focus onto peripheral (sideways) vision this appears to switch the body into the parasympathetic nervous system.

Some martial arts teachers teach their students to use peripheral vision when fighting or sparring. This prevents them from becoming angry and keeps them calm and centred. A variation on this technique is taught to high speed police pursuit drivers.

To benefit from this technique, practise the following exercise:

- Locate a spot on a wall in front of you that is just above eye level. Look at it.
- Begin to put your awareness into the periphery of your vision. What can you see on either side of you?
- Bring up your hands and place them on either side of your head so that you can just see them out of the corner of each eye. Wiggle your fingers as you move them slowly back. This can help you to focus further on your peripheral vision.
- Some people find that imagining an object such as an orange or apple at the top/back of their head helps to increase peripheral vision.
- Expand your peripheral awareness as widely as possible.
- Begin to look around the room whilst keeping peripheral vision.

Spend some time each day practising this technique. It will very swiftly become something you can switch into at will. Once you have mastered it you can use it in any situation to calm yourself and reduce stress levels.

It is, of course, possible to combine this technique with the breathing and self-talk techniques we covered earlier.

Again, if you spend some time practising these techniques you will reap the benefits. Relax!

Unleash The Giant Within

The power of self hypnosis

In this chapter we will be exploring how you can utilise the immense power of hypnosis as a method of performance enhancement. Hypnosis, contrary to the image frequently portrayed on television and in films, is not a strange or esoteric practice. More and more elite sports performers are utilising hypnosis as a powerful method of performance enhancement.

As discussed earlier, we all have not one mind, but two. Or to be more precise, we have two spheres of activity within one mind. So to recap: these are called the conscious mind and the unconscious (sometimes referred to as the subconscious) mind.

Your world view

As described previously, your unconscious mind concentrates on maintaining what is known as your 'world view'. It is your unconscious mind's image of the world. Your world view is a powerful survival tool. For example, your world view tells you that if you step off a cliff you will hurt or kill yourself. This world view protects you from danger by preventing you from falling every time you are on a cliff top.

Once your unconscious mind has established a coherent world view it is reluctant to allow in any data in that may conflict with it. It will therefore accept or reject information depending upon other information that it holds.

The powerful technique of hypnosis can help you to change the content of your unconscious mind so that it better supports you in achieving what you want.

The secret power of hypnosis

It is a useful analogy to think of the mind as the sea. Like the sea it ebbs and flows with the tide. When you are wide awake the unconscious mind is at its lowest ebb. When you are asleep the unconscious mind submerges the conscious mind. In between these two states when you are relaxed, drowsy or sleepy the unconscious tide is high but you can retain conscious awareness. At these times you can literally programme positive new data into the unconscious data bank. When you awake from this state to full consciousness, the new data is stored in the unconscious and is being acted upon.

On a day-to-day basis we experience many different states of consciousness. The brainwave activity in each of these states of consciousness has a unique pattern that can be measured. Brainwaves change frequencies based upon the neural activity in the brain.

Brainwaves are electromagnetic wave forms that are produced by the electrical and chemical activity of the brain. They can be measured with sensitive electronic equipment called an electro-encephalogram. Brainwave frequencies are measured in cycles per second or Hertz and fall into four broad bands:

BETA - 13 to 30 Hertz

Beta waves are most commonly associated with normal, wide awake states in which we are focused on external stimuli. Beta is increased during times of stress, enabling us to manage situations and solve problems.

ALPHA - 7 to 13 Hertz

Alpha waves indicate an alert state with a quiet mind. In the alpha state, attention may be focused outwards or inwards. Alpha may be dominant in states of focused concentration or in attaining a still inner centre.

Increased Alpha has been found to be present in the brainwave patterns of people who practise activities such as meditation, yoga and tai chi. This is one of the brainwave states that we will be utilising when practising self hypnosis.

THETA - 3 to 7 Hertz

Theta waves reflect a state of mind that is attuned with visualisation and creative inspiration. Theta waves tend to be produced during activities such as daydreaming or deep meditation. Theta is also a brainwave state we will be utilising when practising self-hypnosis.

DELTA - 0.1 to 3 Hertz

Delta waves are associated with the deepest levels of physical relaxation. Delta is the slowest of the brainwave frequencies and is associated with dreamless sleep.

What is Hypnosis?

The hypnotic state of mind, or state of awareness, is one in which the unconscious mind is dominant. The process of hypnosis is a way of inducing an unconsciously responsive state of mind.

During a hypnotic procedure (which can be induced by a hypnotist or by you yourself) you will experience changes in sensations, perceptions, thoughts or behaviour.

Although there are many different hypnotic inductions, most include suggestions for relaxation, calmness and well-being. Instructions to imagine or think about pleasant experiences are also commonly included in hypnotic inductions.

People respond to hypnosis in different ways. Some describe their experience as an altered state of consciousness. Others describe hypnosis as a normal state of focused attention, in which people feel very calm and relaxed. Most people describe the experience as very pleasant.

There is evidence of hypnosis or hypnotic-like phenomena in many ancient cultures. The modern history of hypnosis began in the late 1700s with a French physician called Anton Mesmer, who gave his name to the term 'mesmerism'.

In the 1800s, British doctors began to explore the use of hypnosis in healing and as an anaesthetic in surgery.

In more modern times hypnosis continued to be of great interest. In the 1950s both the American Medical Association and the British Medical Society adopted a policy statement that recognised hypnosis as a useful and legitimate treatment in both medicine and dentistry.

Hypnotic suggestion can alter hypnotised subjects' heart rates and anaesthetise parts of their bodies. It can cause skin to blister when a hypnotised subject is touched with a piece of ice and told that it is a piece of red hot metal and, perhaps less dramatically, allow you to change any and every facet of your mind and behaviour.

How to hypnotise yourself

To begin your exploration into hypnosis it is useful to select a place that is personal and as quiet as possible. Somewhere indoors is probably best when first learning self-hypnosis.

The place you choose should be comfortable, safe and as free from interruptions as possible. As you become more proficient you will be able to hypnotise yourself almost anywhere.

You may wish to allow about 15 to 20 minutes for the first few times you practise. As you become more skilled at entering trance, you may find that you only need five to 10 minutes for a session.

The more work you want to do in your self-hypnosis sessions and the more complex your goals, the longer you may want to spend in your trance. Some people prefer a relaxed sitting position and others prefer to lie down. Lying down can make it easier to drift off to sleep when you are in a very relaxed state.

The most important thing is to be as comfortable as possible. Sit or lie down comfortably, using pillows and cushions if you wish. If lying down, keep your legs uncrossed and have your arms lying alongside your body. If sitting, again keep your legs uncrossed, and place your arms at your sides or let them relax in your lap.

Once you are feeling comfortable, start by taking a deep breath. Hold it for second or so and then let it out with a deep sigh. Relax and let go. Repeat this several times. Imagine all your worries and tensions being breathed out of your body as you exhale. As you do this, close your eyes.

Imagine yourself in a beautiful natural environment such as in a tranquil garden or a beautiful meadow or on a beach. Imagine a bright, warm, yellow sun shining upon you. Feel the warm light of the sun and relax even further. Keep breathing slowly, deeply and easily.

Now focus the light upon your right leg. Imagine the sunlight gently penetrating the skin and muscles and deeply relaxing the leg. Count down from 10 to one and with each number you count you will feel your leg relaxing more and more. Slowly count your leg down to full relaxation. When you reach the number one, say to yourself.

'Totally and completely relaxed'.

Repeat this counting down process for your left leg, lower body, both of your arms, upper body, shoulders and neck, scalp and then finally your face. When you are feeling totally relaxed say to yourself,

'I am now going to count from 10 down to one. With every number I count I will become 10 times more relaxed than before, going deeper and deeper into a relaxed hypnotic state.'

Then count down and say,

'10, nine… going down… eight, seven six… deeply relaxed… five, four… going down, down, down… three deeply and totally relaxed… two deeper and deeper, one… totally and completely relaxed. I am now deeply and totally relaxed. At this relaxed level of mind my unconscious mind is open and receptive to the following positive suggestions which it will accept totally and act upon.'

You can now use whatever positive suggestions you choose. These can really be around any aspect of your life that you wish.

Examples could include mental toughness, learning easily, success in competitions and tournaments, feeling calm and relaxed before important events, self-confidence, self-belief and so on.

Some example scripts are:

> 'When I go to compete, I feel a great surge of dynamic energy welling up inside me... a feeling of total self-confidence in my ability to win... calm and confident in the knowledge that I am going to win. I am going to beat my opponents and I am going to enjoy every minute of it.'

> 'If I want to boost my confidence and power before a competition all I have to do is to close my eyes... count from one to five and think of the word **power**... and when I do this I will find that my energy and confidence is boosted... so that when I begin to perform, I will have a real surge in confidence and power.'

> 'I have total confidence in my abilities and I know that I have the ability to be the best. I believe in myself and my abilities. I know that I am becoming more confident every single day.'

> 'I have complete control over my feelings, emotions and thoughts. I have complete control over myself and my performance. I can maintain total focus and total concentration.'

> 'With every passing day I am adopting a more positive attitude and outlook. In this positive state of mind I will experience wonderful new feelings of confidence and strength. I look forward to new challenges with confidence.'

> 'Any barriers or obstacles to exceptional performance have been eliminated. I look forward to every day, secure in the knowledge of my own abilities and of the vast potential within me for future development. Nothing is holding me back any longer and I am completely free to develop all the vast potential within me to its fullest extent.'

> '*I make sure that I get all the rest that I require to perform exceptionally. I am able to sleep soundly and well. I will not waste time worrying about my past or future performances, for each time I practise I will feel myself improving.*'

> '*I see myself performing precisely as I desire. Strong, calm, poised, alert, competent, agile, comfortable, self-assured, commanding. I accept no limitations, for there are none. I demonstrate complete mastery and excellence.*'

When you have completed this stage of your self-hypnosis it is time to bring yourself out of trance.

Say to yourself:

> '*I will now count from one to 10. When I count 10 I will open my eyes. I will feel wide awake, relaxed and happy with positive energy flowing throughout my entire body... one, two, three... coming up now... four, five, six... beginning to wake up... seven, eight... moving and stretching, remembering the situation in this room, nine, 10... wide awake and fully alert, feeling happy and glad to be alive!*'

After such a session you will feel tremendous! People who hypnotise themselves for the first time usually can't wait to do it again. Aside from the positive benefits from the suggestions themselves, hypnosis also has the side benefits of relaxation and stress control.

You can easily combine self-hypnosis and mental rehearsal. The two techniques are very similar. When you are in a trance, mental rehearsal combined with positive suggestions is a very powerful combination.

Despite all the popular misconceptions and misunderstandings that surround it, self-hypnosis is really a very easy skill to master.

As with all skills it is important to practise. I would recommend a practice session every day. In a relatively short time you will be able to put yourself into trance very easily. It will not take long before you start to notice the positive changes manifesting themselves in your life.

Hypnosis is now a mainstream, modern training technique that is used by many elite athletes and business people. It is not the submissive state that you see in films, on television or being demonstrated by stage hypnotists.

It can be used to sharpen your mental focus, relax your body, visualise success, stimulate healing and control your emotions. It is a very powerful technique that will assist you in many areas of your life.

Think Like A Champion

The five empowering beliefs of champions and winners

In this chapter we will be exploring further the fascinating area of beliefs and how they affect our performance. We will also be taking a look at how you can change beliefs that are limiting you. We will conclude this session by understanding the five empowering beliefs that all champions and winners possess.

> 'Man is what he believes.'
> **ANTON CHEKHOV**

The beliefs that we have strongly influence our behaviour. They also motivate us and shape what we do. The beliefs that we hold about ourselves, about other people and the world around us, will exert a powerful influence over our performance in every single area of our lives.

> 'We are what we think. All that we are arises with our thoughts. With our thoughts we make our world.'
> **BUDDHA**

What are beliefs?

Beliefs are essentially judgements and evaluations about ourselves as individuals, other people and the world that we live in. Beliefs are our guiding principles, the inner 'maps' we use to make sense of the world. They can give stability and continuity.

Most of us share some basic beliefs about the world we live in. The majority of people on the planet believe that our earth is round. However, I am reliably informed that there exists a society for people who still think that the earth is flat!

As amusing as this may seem, you do not have to go very far back in history to find a time when most people believed that the earth was flat and that the sun and planets revolved around the earth.

Many of our beliefs are very helpful and useful. We believe that fire burns and that broken glass is sharp. Therefore we avoid exposing our bodies to hot flames and don't step onto broken glass in our bare feet.

Beliefs can be thought of as generalisations about what causes certain things to happen, what things mean and the boundaries in the world around us, in our behaviour and our capabilities.

Beliefs can affect our behaviour. For example, depending upon which belief you have:

'Success requires hard work'

or

'Success is mainly a matter of luck'

...your approach to attempting to reach success will be affected!

Where do our beliefs come from?

Our beliefs can come from a variety of sources. They can come from the way we were brought up, from observing and copying significant people in our lives (such as our parents), from past events that have scared or traumatised us, or from repetitive experiences. We build our beliefs by having an experience of the world and other people and generalising it.

We may currently believe some things as a result of what we were told when we were growing up. When you were young you had no way of knowing if these things were true or not. The expectations of those around us during our childhood can instil beliefs. Some of these beliefs may persist and influence you to this day.

When we believe something, we act as if it is true. This makes it very difficult to disprove. Our beliefs act as very powerful filters on what we perceive.

What the thinker thinks... the prover proves

As Dr. Leonard Orr noted, the human mind behaves if it were divided into two parts, "the thinker" and "the prover". The thinker is very flexible, and can think any number of things. The thinker can think the earth is flat, the thinker can think the earth is round. The thinker can think pretty much anything.

The prover, however, is far more predictable. Whatever the thinker is thinking, the prover will search and sort for evidence to support the belief. If someone believes that they lack intelligence (perhaps from comments made to them by their parents or teachers) then the prover will find evidence to support that.

Information that supports the belief will be noted and evidence that contradicts the belief may be ignored or deleted. In this way beliefs can become a self-fulfilling prophecy.

Beliefs are very powerful and help us to get a sense of certainty and direction in a world that can be anything but predictable. Beliefs can become so powerful that we don't remember that they are not necessarily true – but we behave as if they are. Beliefs are not just 'maps' of what happened in the past – we also use them as 'blueprints' for our future actions.

It is important that you realise the tremendous impact your beliefs can have. One of the most powerful examples of the power of beliefs is the placebo effect.

The placebo effect

A placebo is a blank or inert sample that is sometimes used in trials for new drugs and medicines. A group of people participating in the trial will be given the actual drug or medicine. A control group will be given a placebo – it appears to be the drug but is in fact a pill or substance with no medicinal properties.

Scientifically speaking, it should have no effect upon the person taking it. However, the startling fact is that studies consistently show that about 30% of people respond to placebos as if they are being given the actual drug.

The Pygmalion effect

Perhaps even more startling than the placebo effect is the fact that our beliefs about other people can actually affect their performance.

Several decades ago, Dr Robert Rosenthall of Harvard University conducted over 300 experiments based upon what he called his 'Expectation theory'. [51] [52] In 1971[53] Rosenthall ran an experiment in which he told a group of students that he had developed a strain of super-intelligent rats that could run mazes quickly. He then passed out perfectly normal rats at random, telling half of the students that they had the new 'maze-bright' rats and the other half that they had 'maze-dull' rats.

The rats believed to be bright improved daily in running the maze. They ran faster and more accurately. The 'dull' rats refused to move from the starting point 29% of the time, while the 'bright' rats refused only 11% of the time.

Rosenthal concluded that some students unknowingly communicated high expectations to the supposedly bright rats. The other students communicated low expectations to the supposedly dull ones.

Rosenthal observed, 'Those who believed they were working with intelligent animals liked them better and found them more pleasant. Such students said they felt more relaxed with the animals, they treated them more gently and were more enthusiastic about the experiment than the students who thought they had dull rats to work with.'

51   Rosenthal, R., & Rubin, D. B. (1978). Interpersonal expectancy effects: The first 345 studies. *The Behavioral and Brain Sciences*
52   Rosenthal, R. (1974). *On the Social Psychology of the Self-Fulfilling Prophecy: Further Evidence for Pygmalion Effects and their Mediating Mechanisms.* MSS Modular
53   Rosenthal, R., & Lawson, R. (1964). A longitudinal study of the effects of experimenter bias on the operant learning of laboratory rats. *Journal of Psychiatric Research*

The phenomena that Rosenthal researched is also referred to as the 'Pygmalion effect'. It takes its name from the ancient myth told by Ovid in the tenth book of *Metamorphoses* of the sculptor Pygmalion.

He sought to create an ivory statue of the ideal woman. The result, which he named Galatea, was so beautiful that Pygmalion fell desperately in love with his own creation. He prayed to the goddess Venus to bring Galatea to life. Venus granted his prayer and the couple lived happily ever after.

This myth gave its name to George Bernard Shaw's play *Pygmalion*, in which Professor Henry Higgins insists that he can take a cockney flower girl and, with some vigorous training, pass her off as a duchess.

Further evidence of the Pygmalion effect is revealed in one of Rosenthal's most famous experiments. In 1968,[54] Rosenthal conducted a study using the children from 18 classrooms, three at each of the six grade levels, at a school in San Francisco. All the children in the study were administered a non-verbal test of intelligence, which was disguised as a test that would predict intellectual 'blooming'.

Within each grade level, the three classrooms were composed of children with above-average ability, average ability and below average ability respectively. Within each of the 18 classrooms approximately 20% of the children were chosen at random to form the experimental group.

The teachers of these children were told that their scores on the 'Test of Inflected Acquisition' indicated that they would show surprising gains in intellectual competence during the next eight months of school. The only difference between the experimental group and the control group of children, then, was in the minds of the teachers.

At the end of the school year, eight months later, all the children were retested with the same test of intelligence. Overall the children from whom the teachers had been led to expect greater intellectual gain, showed a significantly greater gain than the children in the control group.

54   Rosenthal, R., & Jacobson, L. (1968). *Pygmalion in the Classroom*. Holt, Rinehart and Winston.

I believe that there are two major considerations from the research into expectancy theory. Firstly, it provides an illustration of how some of your current beliefs may have been shaped by the expectations of significant people in your life such as parents and teachers. Their expectations of you will have influenced you.

Where these were positive you may have a corresponding set of positive beliefs; where these were perhaps less positive, you may have some beliefs that are not so supportive and helpful.

Dr Richard Bandler, the co-founder of NLP (Neuro Linguistic Programming), makes the point that people make the mistake of confusing their belief systems with reality. That is, they believe their beliefs to be true and act accordingly.

Our beliefs become a self-fulfilling prophecy

The notion of the self-fulfilling prophecy was conceptualised by Robert Merton, a professor of sociology at Columbia University. Merton said the phenomenon occurs when 'a false definition of the situation evokes a new behaviour which makes the original false conception come true'.

We anticipate how something which has not yet happened will be in the future and this affects how we behave in the present.

The future reaches backwards to affect the present. For example, what's the point of an individual trying if they believe their efforts to succeed are bound to fail; that the outcome is a foregone conclusion?

On the other hand when you expect to succeed, the energy and optimism generated may help with performance and make you more likely to succeed. Therefore your beliefs about the future help create the very future they anticipate.

It used to be believed that it was impossible to run a mile in under four minutes. It was not until 1954 when Roger Bannister broke this physical and psychological barrier that this belief changed. In the next three decades over 12 individual athletes ran a mile in under four minutes. People's beliefs had changed and their performances changed too.

I believe it is more constructive to consider not whether your beliefs are true or false, but whether they are helpful or not. The good news is that from now on you will be able to exercise some choice over your beliefs and choose beliefs that support you in getting what you want. We will explore ways to do this shortly.

The second consideration from expectancy theory applies to the relationship between managers, leaders, teachers, coaches and their students. From the research into expectancy theory, we can see that teachers, for example, with high expectations of their students will have students who perform better.

If you are a manager/leader/teacher/coach/parent then you should consider this matter deeply.

As discussed, we build beliefs by generalising from our experience of the world and other people. We believe what we are told when we are young because we have no way of testing, and these beliefs may persist and remain unmodified by later achievements.

Beliefs are a powerful influence on our lives. Our beliefs about ourselves and what is possible greatly impact on our effectiveness. When we believe something, we act as if it is true. As Henry Ford is quoted as saying 'If you think you can or you think you can't – you are right'.

You may wish to consider how your own personal beliefs support or limit you in achieving what it is you want. Beliefs can be changed (at some stage in their lives many people have believed in the existence of Santa Claus and the Tooth Fairy!) and limiting beliefs changed to empowering beliefs.

Many of our beliefs are very helpful and useful. I mentioned that we believe that fire burns and that broken glass is sharp. Therefore, we avoid exposing our bodies to hot flames and don't step onto broken glass in our bare feet.

However, in the course of my experiments into beliefs I have done both of these things! I have walked over a 20-foot bed of coals burning at 1200 degrees Fahrenheit in my bare feet and not been burnt.

With the correct supervision and training this feat can be accomplished by most people. The ability to do this is easily explained by physics. However, it requires a belief change to actually take that first step onto the burning coals.

I have also walked in my bare feet along a 20-foot bed of razor-sharp broken glass. The glass bed was made by smashing over 1000 wine bottles. Again this feat can be accomplished by most people if they have the correct training and supervision, and again physics can explain how it is possible. As with fire walking, it does require a belief change for you to be able place your bare foot into the bed of broken glass for the first time.

I must stress that events such as fire and glass walking must only be undertaken after adequate training from suitably qualified and insured instructors. If certain specific procedures are not followed, people can get badly burnt or cut.

I use fire and glass walking as metaphors when talking to people about beliefs. They show that some of the beliefs we have are not based on any form of truth. Limiting beliefs can be changed to beliefs that support us.

How to change beliefs

Here is a simple process that you can follow to help you to change limiting beliefs:

Write down a list of three beliefs that have been limiting you. Sometimes, just the process of writing them down can allow you to begin to realise that they are not true. As you look at these beliefs, you may become aware that, at one point in time, they were in some way useful in helping you to make sense of the world. But perhaps now, rather like believing in the tooth fairy, they've passed their use-by-date.

Underneath each belief, write the heading 'Evidence'. Start the process of finding the evidence that these beliefs are false. Leave decision and judgement to one side. Just write the evidence on the evidence list.

Write down a list of three beliefs that would be useful and empowering and that will help you achieve your goals, or are beliefs that you'd just like to believe. State them positively.

Underneath your three new empowering beliefs write the heading 'Evidence' and start to find the evidence that these beliefs are true. When evidence is presented, leave decision and judgement to one side. Just write the evidence on the evidence list.

Pretend that the new positive beliefs are true. As bizarre as this may sound to you, when you behave in this way amazing things will happen.

If you consider that none of your limiting beliefs are really 'true' and that you probably didn't realise that you were choosing them, then the only logical course of action is to choose some different beliefs that support and empower you. Act as if they are true for 21 days and then notice what has changed. You will be amazed at the difference.

Once Roger Bannister changed people beliefs about the four minute mile, people started to act as if it was possible to run a mile in under four minutes, and they succeeded.

Some other belief change methodologies that you may like to explore include:

Mental Rehearsal

The brain cannot tell the difference between a vividly imagined event and a real event. Therefore, mentally rehearsing a desired state or ability can make it believable to the brain.

Affirmation

The verbalising of positive statements to oneself is an established technique for belief change ('Every day in every way I am getting better and better'). The time just before and immediately after sleep are particularly recommended for affirmation as the brain is particularly receptive at these times to suggestion.

Hypnosis

Hypnosis works by getting people into a relaxed and receptive state of mind and then making positive suggestions directly to their unconscious minds. This can be achieved through self-hypnosis (see the previous chapter) or by visiting a hypnotherapist.

We are not born with beliefs in the same way we are born with eye or hair colour. Beliefs can change and develop. Beliefs can be a matter of choice. You can drop beliefs that limit you and build beliefs that make your life more enjoyable and successful.

Empowering beliefs allow you to find out what could be possible and how capable a person you really are.

In the course of my research I have modelled a number of generalised beliefs that elite performers in any field possess. You may wish to explore these beliefs for yourself. Perhaps you might like to make these five beliefs your affirmations that you repeat morning and night and throughout the day.

Maybe you would like to act as if these beliefs are true for you for 21 days and see how much your life has changed for the better.

The five empowering beliefs of champions and winners

'I Can Do This'
This relates to an individual's sense of self-confidence and self-efficacy and also that they have the personal resources and abilities available to succeed.

'I Like Myself'
This relates to an individual having a sense of self-worth and self-liking. A high level of self-esteem will contribute positively to self-confidence – a major differentiating factor between elite and non-elite performers.

'I Am Responsible'

This relates to the individual taking ownership of themselves and their responses in relation to events that occur. The individual could be described as having 'an internal locus of causality' and sufficient levels of intrinsic motivation.

'I Know What I Want'

This relates to the individual having a clear goal for specifically what it is that they want to achieve, and this is proven to enhance performance and support concentration and attention control.

'I Am Committed To Getting What I Want'

This relates to the individual backing their desired goal with the necessary motivation to achieve it. The evidence suggests that elite performers will select more difficult goals to which they are highly committed. This also relates to an individual combining their goal commitment with persistence and effort. The evidence relating to elite performers states that they will increase their level of persistence and effort when their goals are not achieved.

Amazing things can happen when you start behaving as if your new empowering beliefs are true. Start believing!

> 'In the province of the mind what one believes to be true either is true or becomes true, within certain limits to be found experientially or experimentally. These limits are further beliefs to be transcended. In the province of the mind there are no limits.'
> **DR JOHN LILLY**

Getting Into The Zone

The psychology of peak performance

As described at the beginning of this book, peak performance has been described as 'behaviour that exceeds one's average performance' or 'an episode of superior functioning'.

Peak performance is about going beyond what you think is currently possible. It may not necessarily be about being better than other people. It is about being the very best that you can be and will often result in a 'personal best' performance.

Please do not make the mistake of thinking that peak performance is confined solely to some small group of sporting legends or martial arts masters. Peak performance is more likely to occur when your skill level matches the demand or challenge of the situation and this means that peak performance can be attained at whatever level someone is working at.

Being in the zone

The particular state of mind that often accompanies episodes of superior functioning and peak performance is sometimes described as 'being in the zone' or the 'flow' state.

In this state there is a total immersion in the activity one is engaged in, one feels in total control and performance is effortless. You are not thinking about your performance and there is no fear of failure. Time often appears to slow down and the universe appears to be integrated and unified. An interesting description of this state is described by the Japanese sword master, Takuan:

> 'When the swordsman stands against his opponent, he is not to think of the opponent, nor of himself, nor of his enemy's sword movements. He just stands there with his sword, which, forgetful of all technique, is ready only to allow the dictates of the unconscious. The man has effaced himself as the wielder of the sword. When he strikes, it is not the man but the sword in the hand of the unconscious that strikes.'

When athletes are asked to describe their 'greatest moments', the following perceptions are often described:

- A loss of fear – there was no fear of failure.
- The athletes were not thinking about their performance.
- The athletes were totally immersed in what they were doing.
- The athletes had a narrow focus of attention.
- Performance was effortless.
- The athletes felt in complete control.
- They experienced some time and/or space distortion, with time usually seeming to slow down
- The universe appeared to be integrated and unified.

The peak performance state has also been described as 'being possessed yet in total control' and experiencing 'profound intensity, total concentration and an enthusiasm that bordered on joy'.[55]

Flow

Often associated with peak performance is the state called flow. It is the state in which people are 'so involved in an activity that nothing else seems to matter'.[56] Flow is not analogous to peak performance. One may be in flow and not necessarily be experiencing peak performance. However, when an athlete experiences peak performance, they often appear to be in a flow state.

It has been suggested that flow may be a precursor to or the psychological process underlying peak performance.

When athletes are in flow, they experience the following nine dimensions which are very similar to the athlete's perceptions on their 'greatest moments in sport' described above.

1. The challenge of the situation matches the skills of the athlete, and these challenges and skills are at a personal high level.

2. Awareness and action merge, so that movement is perceived as effortless and the athlete 'ceases to be aware of him/herself as separate from her/his action'.

55   Loehr, J.E. (1984) How to overome stress and play at your peak all the time. *Tennis*
56   Ravizza, K. (1977) Peak experience in sport. *Journal of Humanistic Psychology*

3. Goals are clear; 'there is clarity about what one is to do'.

4. Unambiguous feedback indicates that what is being done is correct.

5. Total and complete concentration on the task at hand occurs.

6. There is a paradox of control, or the sense of being in complete control without actively attempting to be in control. This has also been described as a clear sense of being in control of performance so that it feels effortless and without fear of failure.

7. Loss of self-consciousness whereby one is aware of performing but is not concerned with self-evaluation.

8. A transformation of time in which time may seem to speed up or slow down.

1. An 'autotelic' experience in which the activity is enjoyable and participation becomes its own reward. [57]

How to get into the zone

It is not possible to force yourself into the zone. You have to encourage and welcome this very specific state of mind, inviting it, rather than commanding it.

This state of mind is paradoxical. The very moment you realise that you are in the zone you will have come out of it. It is not possible to be in the zone and analyse what it feels like at the same time! To think about the zone you have to be outside of it.

When we learn new things (such as driving a car) we go through four stages:

Unconscious Incompetence

At the unconscious incompetence stage you don't know what you don't know how about how to do something. To continue the learning to drive analogy, you don't know what you don't know about the skill of driving..

---

57   Jackson, S.A., & Csikszentmihalyi. (1999) *Flow in sports*, Human Kinetics

Conscious Incompetence

At the conscious incompetence stage, you are now aware that you don't know how to do something. You know that driving requires many skills and that you do not currently possess them.

Conscious Competence

At the conscious competence stage you have learned the skills to carry out the thing you want to do but they require your full and total concentration. You can drive but it requires your complete and conscious awareness to do it correctly.

Unconscious Competence

At the stage of unconscious competence you can drive without thinking about the skills involved in changing gear, steering or accelerating – it all happens automatically.

Part of being in the zone is a letting go, a release of your conscious preparation and letting your unconscious competence take over. You have to let go and trust your unconscious mind. This state of mind is sometimes described as the 'no mind' state.

In this state of mind you will act without conscious effort on your part; what you do will flow easily. Sometimes after such an experience people report almost 'waking up' and coming back to the real world. The state can almost seem trance-like.

You may have experienced something similar to this when driving your car. Have you ever got into your car and driven off, only to 'wake up' a few minutes later realising that you have driven several miles without paying conscious attention to either your driving or where you were going?

This phenomenon is sometimes referred to as 'highway hypnosis'. Driving is quite a complex task, but you were quite safe, you drove the car along the road safely, even though you were not consciously aware but instead in a type of trance state. If there had been any sort of dangerous situation then you would have suddenly 'woken up'.

It is possible to trust your unconscious mind – with your life in the case of driving - to run your many body functions, as it is doing perfectly right now, and to help you achieve peak performance.

The subject of brainwave activity was covered earlier but let us revisit this subject again as it relates to getting into the peak performance state.

Throughout our lives, we experience many different states of consciousness. Each of these states of consciousness has a unique pattern of brainwaves that can be measured and mapped. Brainwaves are electromagnetic wave forms that are produced by the electrical and chemical activity of the brain. They can be measured with sensitive electronic equipment; they change frequencies based upon the neural activity in the brain.

Whilst the subject of brainwave frequency is complex, it can be useful to think about the practical utilisation of what we understand about the 4 bands of Beta, Alpha, Theta and Delta mentioned earlier.

From the assembled evidence, it seems plausible that an alpha brainwave state would be associated with being in the peak performance state. Therefore, practising getting yourself into this brainwave state through the use of self-hypnosis and meditation is recommended. The more you practise the easier it will be for you to consciously 'slip into' an Alpha brainwave state.

How to achieve the peak performance state

To achieve the special peak performance state you will need to let go. You will need to trust yourself and trust the countless hours of physical and mental preparation you have completed.

Getting into the zone, or achieving the peak performance state cannot be something you force yourself to do; rather it is something you allow to happen, something you surrender to.

However, there are some things that you can be aware of that will assist you in the achievement of this very special state:

- Make sure you are very clear about your objectives and goals. You need to have total clarity about what you are going to do.
- Ensure the challenge of the situation matches your current level of skill, and that these challenges and skills are at a high personal level.

- Do not concern yourself with succeeding or failing, winning or losing.
  - Feel highly confident about your ability to perform.
  - Trust yourself that you can perform perfectly.
  - Do not think about how you are performing, just immerse yourself into it, concentrate fully upon the act of doing, not how you are doing.
  - Remain mentally calm.
  - Focus your energy fully into your performance.
  - Remain optimistic and positive.
  - Enjoy yourself!

Research shows that the probability of good and potentially peak performance can be substantially increased if the following combination of good feelings could be triggered and maintained:

- High energy (challenge, inspiration, determination, intensity).
- Fun and enjoyment.
- No pressure (low anxiety).
- Optimism and positivity.
- Mental calmness.
- Confidence.
- Being very focused.
- Being in control.[58]

In conclusion, people who focus their attention fully on the task at hand, control their anxiety, and have appropriate and challenging goals will be more likely to experience being in the zone or achieving the peak performance state more often.

The psychological strategies and techniques you have learned in *The Inner Winner* will assist you in achieving this peak performance state. This is one of the most exciting concepts that you will ever encounter in your quest to become a true master of whatever field you have chosen to dedicate yourself to. I wish you every success is achieving this unique state of mind on a frequent and regular basis.

58   Ravizza, K. (1977) Peak experience in sport. *Journal of Humanistic Psychology*

Putting It All Together

How to combine your psychological tactics and strategies for maximum effect

We have covered a lot of important information in this book. Let's now review several of the key psychological methods that contribute to improved performance through achieving psychological states such as increased confidence and reduced anxiety. The methods we have identified could be considered as psychological skills in their own right.

Goal-setting

Psychological research on goal-setting is considerable. It has been conducted in a variety of laboratory and field settings, has used a wide variety of tasks (many from outside the world of sport) and has employed diverse samples (including school children, manual labourers, managers and scientists).

The most important result generated from the research is that goal-setting clearly and consistently facilitates enhanced performance. A review of well over 100 studies on goal-setting concluded that 'the beneficial effect of goal-setting on task performance is one of the most robust and replicable findings in the psychological literature. 90% of the studies showed positive or partially positive effects. Furthermore, these effects are found just as reliable in the field settings as in the laboratory'.[59]

Goal-setting can also contribute positively to a number of key psychological skills such as self-confidence, self-efficacy, motivation, coping with adversity, concentration and attention control. In addition, goals are a key factor identified in the achievement of the peak performance 'flow' state.

59   Locke, E.A., and Latham, G.P. (1990) *A Theory of Goal Setting and Task Performance*, Prentice-Hall

Imagery and Mental Rehearsal

According to psychological research, over 99% of the Olympic athletes surveyed used imagery and mental rehearsal.[60] In addition elite athletes have also been reported as being more proficient at imagery and mental rehearsal than non-elite performers.

Imagery can be defined as a symbolic sensory experience that may occur in any sensory mode. It has been defined as an 'awareness of quasi-sensory and quasi-perceptual experiences under conditions where the actual stimuli that produced the real sensorial and perceptual experiences are absent'.[61] As such, imagery is a mental process or a mode of thought.

Mental rehearsal, on the other hand, is defined here as the employment of imagery to mentally practise an act. Thus mental rehearsal is a technique as opposed to merely a mental process.

Psychological research concludes that there are two very important conclusions regarding mental rehearsal:

- Mental rehearsal is better than no practice at all.
- Mental rehearsal combined with physical practice is more effective than either alone.
- Imagery and/or mental rehearsal can contribute positively to self-confidence, activation, relaxation and coping with adversity.

Self-Talk

You engage in self-talk any time you carry on an internal dialogue with yourself, such as giving yourself instructions and encouragement or interpreting what you are feeling or perceiving. This dialogue can occur out loud or inside your head.

Several researchers have shown that thought content and self-statements are important predictors of sports success. Indeed it has been found that the best discriminator of qualifiers and non-qualifiers for the US Olympic gymnastics team was the nature and content of their self-talk just prior to competition.

---

60   Orlick, T. and Partington, I., (1987) The sport psychology consultant: Analysis of critical components as viewed by Olympic athletes, *The Sport Psychologist*
61   Richardson, A., (1967) Mental Imagery, *Research Quarterly*

Specifically, the successful gymnasts employed positive self-statements whilst the non-qualifiers exhibited negative self-talk.

Self-talk contributes positively to self-efficacy, self-confidence, activation, stress management and coping with adversity.

Relaxation

Most individuals will experience some anxiety during a competitive or important situation. The ability to control that anxiety to manageable proportions and even to use it to their advantage to get a performance edge, distinguishes elite from non-elite performers.

Being relaxed during performance is one characteristic of the peak performance 'flow' state. The ability to achieve a state of relaxation contributes positively to peak performance, coping with adversity, stress management and achieving appropriate states of activation.

State Management

Research demonstrates that elite athletes use a variety of techniques to maintain control over their state of mind and body.

A variety of skills combine to enable state management. These include mental rehearsal, self-talk, anchoring and utilising the mind/body connection.

Self-Hypnosis

Hypnosis is a particular state of mind or state of awareness in which the unconscious mind is dominant.

Hypnosis can be used to change aspects of your mind and behaviour. It can be utilised to change your beliefs about yourself and in this way it can be a powerful facilitator of improved performance.

We will now explore how these psychological skills can be combined together.

A Unified Model of Peak Performance Psychology

The various psychological skills discussed above are combined in a 'Unified Model of Peak Performance Psychology' which is illustrated later in this chapter.

Throughout this book we have examined separate components such as self-confidence, motivation and coping with adversity. However, people are not simple one-dimensional beings – they are multivariate and complex, meaning thatin any one person at anny one time, all the psychological factors we have discussed (and others that we have not) are operating simultaneously.

In addition, people do not live in a vacuum; they function within a highly complex social and organisational environment that exerts influences on them and their performance.

The topics and variables that have been discussed in the various chapters of this book have been combined into a unifying model of psychological preparation for peak performance, so that the relationships between them and the social-organisational environment can be understood.

At the core of the model are the various neurological levels. These are drawn from the field of psychology called Neuro Linguistic Programming.

In our brain structure and language there are natural hierarchies or levels of experience. These are known as neurological levels. The effect of each level is to organise and control the information on the level below it. Changing something on an upper level, such as our beliefs and values, will change things on a lower level like our skills and capabilities. Thus our beliefs about our abilities will exert a powerful effect upon our skills and capabilities, our behaviour and therefore our results. However, changing something on a lower level would not necessarily affect the upper levels and a specific instance of behaviour may not affect our skills and capabilities or beliefs about ourselves.

The neurological levels model provides a useful way of 'chunking down' the various aspects of performance psychology, without losing sight of the unified whole.

The various levels of the model are explained as follows:

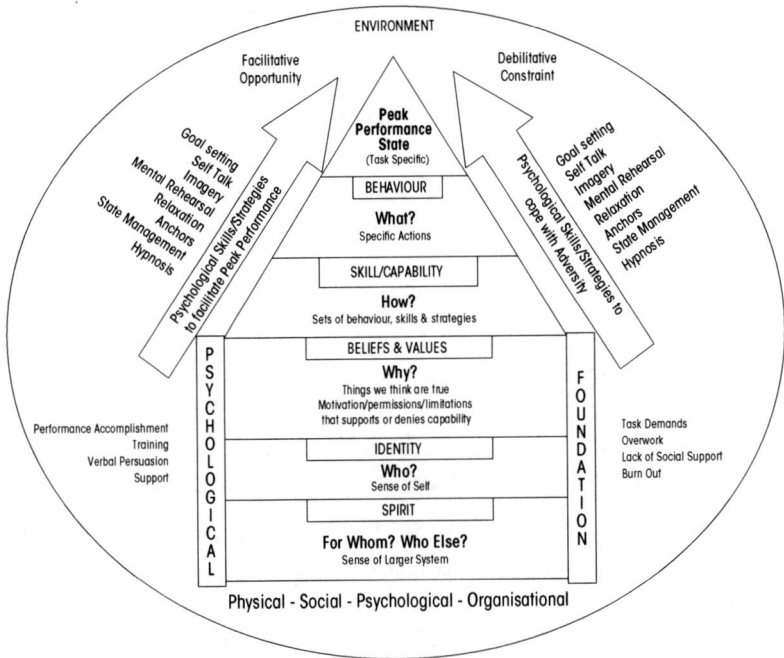

ENVIRONMENT

Facilitative Opportunity

Debilitative Constraint

Peak Performance State (Task Specific)

BEHAVIOUR

What? Specific Actions

SKILL/CAPABILITY

How? Sets of behaviour, skills & strategies

BELIEFS & VALUES

Why? Things we think are true Motivation/permissions/limitations that supports or denies capability

IDENTITY

Who? Sense of Self

SPIRIT

For Whom? Who Else? Sense of Larger System

Goal setting, Self Talk, Imagery, Mental Rehearsal, Relaxation, Anchors, State Management, Hypnosis

Psychological Skills Strategies to facilitate Peak Performance

Goal setting, Self Talk, Imagery, Mental Rehearsal, Relaxation, Anchors, State Management, Hypnosis

Psychological Skills Strategies to cope with Adversity

PSYCHOLOGICAL

FOUNDATION

Performance Accomplishment Training Verbal Persuasion Support

Task Demands Overwork Lack of Social Support Burn Out

Physical - Social - Psychological - Organisational

ENVIRONMENT

You operate within an environment. This is represented by the oval, which is the boundary of the model. Environment is the specific external conditions within which your behaviour takes place.

Factors that may be apparent in the environment could be physical (e.g. the various characteristics of the hall where a sporting tournament is taking place), social (e.g. the people involved), organisational (e.g. the club or organisation you are part of) and psychological.

These factors will be a blend of facilitative and debilitative; opportunities and constraints. In simple terms, they will either be helpful or unhelpful to your performance.

For example, the model makes reference to specific facilitative factors that may exist in the environment (performance accomplishments you experience, training you have done, verbal persuasion from your coach/team, mates' support from the crowd) and specific debilitative factors in the environment (task demands, overwork, lack of social support, burn out).

THE PSYCHOLOGICAL FOUNDATION

The rectangle at the base of the model contains your psychological foundation. It can be thought of as your unique and essential nature. This consists of three elements:

Spirit

This is your sense of yourself as you interact with a larger system and relates to the fact that we all part of a larger system that reaches beyond ourselves to our family, community and the world. It asks 'For Whom?' or 'Who Else?' does the individual interact with, serve or support with reference to a specific goal or outcome.

The word 'spirit', as it is used in the model, does not necessarily have any religious or spiritual connotations, (although this can be important for some people). It is more focused on our inter-relationships with other people and the wider world.

Identity

This is your sense of self. It asks 'Who?' 'Who am I?' and 'What kind of person am I?' in relation to the selected goal or outcome involved. Identity factors determine our overall purpose in life and shape our beliefs and values through our sense of self.

Beliefs/Values

Beliefs and Values provide the reinforcement that supports or denies our capabilities. At this level are the various things we think are true, and used as a basis for daily action. Beliefs can be both permissions and limitations. It asks the question 'Why?', 'Why am I doing this?', 'What values are important to me as I achieve my outcome?', 'What beliefs guide me as I achieve my outcome?' in relation to the selected goal or outcome involved.

Champions and winners frequently possess five empowering beliefs:

1. 'I can do this' – This relates to your sense of self-confidence and self-efficacy and having the personal resources and abilities available to succeed.

2. 'I like myself' – This relates to you having a sense of self-worth and self-liking. A high level of self-esteem will contribute positively to self-confidence – a major differentiating factor between elite and non-elite performers.

3. 'I am responsible' – This relates to you taking ownership of yourself and your responses in relation to events that occur. If you accept responsibility for yourself and your actions then you can be described as having 'an internal locus of causality'. Rather than being at the mercy of external factors, you will draw upon your intrinsic motivation to drive you to achieve what you wish to achieve.

4. 'I know what I want' – This relates to you having a clear goal for specifically what it is that you want to achieve. This is proven to enhance performance and support concentration and attention control.

5. 'I am committed to getting what I want' – This relates to you backing your desired goal with the necessary motivation to achieve it. The evidence suggests that elite performers will select more difficult goals to which they are highly committed. This also relates to an individual combining their goal commitment with persistence and effort. The evidence relating to elite performers indicates that they will increase their level of persistence and effort when their goals are not achieved.

The personal foundation represents your unique psychological makeup, and contains your unique identity, values, beliefs and purpose; it could be thought of as generating your passion. It is the foundation upon which your achievements and accomplishments are built.

As discussed previously, it is possible to alter one's beliefs about oneself using a variety of techniques including the use of affirmations and self-hypnosis.

The next two levels of the model facilitate the manifestation of your unique individual contribution in the environment.

SKILL/CAPABILITY

This relates to the skills and capabilities you possess. It answers the question 'How?' What are the behaviours, skills and strategies that you will use to achieve the outcome in question?

The core psychological skills identified above (goal-setting, self-talk, imagery/mental rehearsal, relaxation, anchors, state management and self-hypnosis) can either facilitate peak performance or help you to cope with stress and adversity.

In many cases the psychological skills will not only help you to cope with adversity but will also simultaneously facilitate enhanced performance. In essence these skills can be thought of as two sides of the same coin.

These skills and strategies are represented by and contained within the two arrows. These skills focus and facilitate your peak performance behaviour.

BEHAVIOUR

This relates to the specific behaviours that you will carry out. It answers the question 'What do I do?' in relation to the specific outcome desired. These behaviours will be a product of all of the levels below.

PEAK PERFORMANCE STATE (task specific)

At the pinnacle of the behaviour level is the task specific peak performance state. This is the culmination of all of the levels below it.

Your essential nature (your sense of the larger system within which you operate and your sense of self) is focused on an outcome that is consistent with your values and is enabled by empowering beliefs.

You will be utilising your psychological training skills to help to produce effective behaviours that will get you the result you want.

After studying *The Inner Winner* and practising the exercises contained within it, you now possess psychological skills and capabilities that allow the expression of your unique self in your chosen field(s).

This can be done by:

- Using the psychological skills to facilitate peak performance
  or

- Using the psychological skills to reduce or prevent debilitative factors.

You can think of this as 'getting out of your own way' and allowing enhanced performance to take place. This enables your behaviour to peak in an appropriate state to deliver the desired outcome as efficiently, effectively and effortlessly as possible.

You may wish to take a goal or outcome that is important to you and plot it through the neurological levels – for example:

- **Peak Performance State (Task Specific)**
  What is the performance state you are seeking?
  e.g. remaining calm and focused during specific situations.

- **Behaviour**
  What specific actions will you need to do?
  e.g. the specific movement and behaviours you will need to demonstrate.

- **Skill/Capability**
  How are you going to achieve this?
  e.g. physical practice, mental rehearsal, self-talk, state management using peripheral vision focus to remain calm and relaxed

- **Beliefs and Values**
  Why are you doing this?
  e.g. you value mastery and achieving your goal will be a demonstration of this. You like yourself and believe in your ability to perform well. You take full and total responsibility for your performance.

- **Identity**
  Who are you when you are doing this?
  e.g. you are a winner, an inspirer, a role model.

- Spirit
  For who else are you doing this?
  e.g. for your partner to repay them for their support, for your parents to make them feel proud, for other people in your organisation by setting a good example to them to follow.

You may wish to experiment with the model yourself. I trust you will find it useful.

Conclusion

The Inner Winner has identified the various factors that facilitate enhanced performance and made a powerful suite of psychological skills available to you.

As with any other skill, these skills must be practised for them to become effective.

If you wish to continue to release and realise more and more of your potential, then I encourage you to spend sufficient time practising these skills.

When mastered they will make a powerful contribution to helping you to create the life you desire and deserve.

I wish you every success!

If I can be of assistance to you in any way then please do make contact.

Simon Hazeldine

References

Bandura, A (1982) Self-efficacy mechanism in human agency, *American Psychologist*

Bandura, A. (1986) *Social Foundations of Thought and Action: A Social Cognitive Theory* Prentice Hall

Beggs, W. (1990) Goal Setting in Sport. In J.G. Jones & L.Hardy(eds), *Stress and Performance* Wiley

Bernard, A., (2010) The effects of self-talk on the level of success of college students

Caudhill, D., et al (1983) Psyching-up and track athletes: a preliminary investigation, *Journal of Sport Psychology*

Clarkson, M., (1999) *Competitive Fire* Human Kinetics

Felts, D.L., & Riessinger, C.A. (1990) Effects of in vivo emotive imagery and performance feedback on self-efficacy and muscular endurance, *Journal of Sport Psychology*

Feltz, D.L. (1984) Self Efficacy as a cognitive mediator of athletic performance. In W.F. Straub (ed.), *Cognitive Sport Psychology*

Feltz, D.L. & Landers, D.M., (1983) The effects of mental practice on motor skill learning and performance: A meta: analysis, *Journal of Sport Psychology*

Feltz, D.L. (1984) Self Efficacy as a cognitive mediator of athletic performance. In W.F. Straub (ed.), *Cognitive Sport Psychology*

Garfield, C., (1985) *Peak Performance: Mental Training Techniques of the World's Greatest Athletes* Warner Books

Glass, C.R., & Merluzzi, T.V., (1981). Cognitive assessment of social evaluative anxiety. In T.V. Merluzzi, C.R. Glass, & M. Genest (Eds.) *Cognitive assessment.* Guildford Press

Goffi, C. (1984) *Tournament Tough* Ebury Press

Gould, D., et al (1981) Psychological characteristics of successful and nonsuccessful Big Ten wrestlers. *Journal of Sport Psychology*

Gould, D., Hodge, K., Peterson, K., & Petlichkoff, L. (1987). Psychological foundations of coaching: Similarities and differences among intercollegiate wrestling coaches. *The Sport Psychologist*

Greenleaf, C., Gould, D., & Diffenbach, K., (2001) Factors Influencing Olympic Performance *Journal of Applied Sports Psychology*

Hackfort, D., Scwenkmezger, P. (1993). Anxiety. In R.N. Singer, M. Murphy & L.K. Tennant (Eds.), *Handbook of research on sport psychology*, Macmillan

Hamilton, S.A., & Fremour, W.J. (1985). Cognitive behavioural training for college basketball free throw performance. *Cognitive Therapy and Research*

Hemery, D. (1991) *Sporting Excellence: What makes a Champion* Harper Collins Willow

Hemery, D. (1986) *The Pursuit Of Sporting Excellence* Willow Books

Highlen, P.S. (1979) Psychological characteristics of successful and nonsuccessful elite wrestlers: An exploratory study. *Journal of Sport Psychology*

Highlen, P.S. (1979) Psychological characteristics of successful and nonsuccessful elite wrestlers: An exploratory study. *Journal of Sport Psychology*

Jackson, S.A., & Csikszentmihalyi. (1999) *Flow in sports* Human Kinetics

Jackson, S.A. & Roberts, G.C. (1992) Positive performance states of athletes: Toward a conceptual understanding of peak performance. *The Sport Psychologist*

Jackson, S.A. (1996) Toward a conceptual understanding of the flow experience in elite athletes. *Research Quarterly for Exercise and Sport*

Jones, G., & Swain, A.B.J. (1995) Predisposition to experience debilitative and facilitative anxiety in elite and non elite performers, *The Sport Psychologist*

Jones, J.G. & Hardy, L. (1990) Stress in sport: Experiences of some elite performers. In G. Jones and L. Hardy (eds), *Stress and Performance in Sport*

Jones, G. (2002) What is this thing called mental toughness? An investigation of elite sports performers. *Journal of Applied Sports Psychology*

Jones, G. (1994) Intensity and interpretation of anxiety symptoms in elite and non-elite sports performers, *Personal Individual Differences*

Jones, G., & Moorhouse, A., (2007) *Developing mental toughness.* Spring Hill

Kingston, K.M., and Hardy, L. (1994) When are some goals more beneficial than others?, *Journal of Sport Sciences*

Locke, E.A. (1968) Towards a theory of task motivation and incentives, *Organisational Behaviour and Human Performance*

Locke, E.A., & Latham, G.P. (1985) The application of goal setting to sport, *Journal of Sport Psychology*

Locke, E.A., & Latham, G.P. (1990) *A theory of goal setting and task performance* Prentice-Hall

Loehr, J.E. (1984) How to overcrome stress and play at your peak all the time. *Tennis*

Lutkus, A.D. (1975) The effect of 'imaging' on mirror drawing, *Bulletin of the Psychonomic Society*

Mahoney, M.J., & Avener, M. (1977) Psychology of the elite athlete: An exploratory study. *Cognitive Therapy and Research*

Mahoney, M.J. (1987) Psychological skills and exceptional athletic performance, *The Sports Psychologist*

Murphy, S.M. (1988) The on-site provision of sport psychology services at the 1987 U.S. Olympic Festival, *The Sport Psychologist*

O'Connor, E.J., & Kirschenbaum, D.S. (1982). Something succeeds like success. Positive self monitoring for unskilled golfers. *Cognitive Therapy and Research*

Orlick, T., and Partington, J. (1987) The sport psychology consultant: Analysis of critical components as viewed by Canadian Olympic athletes, *The Sport Psychologist*

Orlick, T. and Partington, J. (1988) Mental links to excellence, *The Sport Psychologist*

Orlick, T., and Lee-Gartner, K. (1993) Going for the dream and reaching it: The Olympic downhill, *Performance Enhancement*

Orlick, T., (2000) *In pursuit of excellence – how to win in sport and life through mental training* Human Kinetics

Ravizza, K. (1977) Peak experience in sport. *Journal of Humanistic Psychology*

Richardson, A., (1967) Mental Practice: A review and discussion. *Research Quarterly*

Rosenthal, R., & Rubin, D. B. (1978). Interpersonal expectancy effects: The first 345 studies. *The Behavioral and Brain Sciences*

Rosenthal, R. (1974). *On the Social Psychology of the Self-Fulfilling Prophecy: Further Evidence for Pygmalion Effects and their Mediating Mechanisms.*

Rosenthal, R., & Lawson, R. (1964). A longitudinal study of the effects of experimenter bias on the operant learning of laboratory rats. *Journal of Psychiatric Research*

Rosenthal, R., & Jacobson, L. (1968). *Pygmalion in the Classroom.* New York: Holt, Rinehart and Winston.

Seligman, M. (1991) *Learned Optimism* Knopf

Schwartz, R., M., (1986) The internal dialogue: On the asymmetry between positive and negative coping thoughts. *Cognitive Therapy and Research*

Schwartz, R.M., & Gottman, J.M. (1976). Toward a task analysis of assertive behaviour. *Journal of Consulting and Clinical Psychology*

Selye, H., (1974) *Stress without distress* Lippincott Williams & Wilkins

Hardy, L., Jones, G., & Gould, D., (1996) *Understanding psychological preparation for sport – Thoery and practice of elite performers.* Wiley

Van Raalte, J.L., Brewer, B.W., Lewis, B.P., Linder, D.E., Wildman, G., & Kozimor, J. (1995) Cork! The positive effects of positive and negative self-talk and dart performance. *Journal of Sport Behaviour*

Vasta, R., & Brockner, J., (1979). Self-esteem and self-evaluative covert statements. *Journal of Consulting and Clinical Psychology* Weinberg, R.S., Smith, J., Jackson,A., & Gould,D. (1984). Effect of association, dissociation and positive self-talk strategies on endurance performance. *Canadian Journal of Applied Sports Sciences*

Williams, J., (Ed). (2001) *Applied Sports Psychology Personal Growth to Peak Performance* Mayfield

Simon Hazeldine MSc, FInstSMM

"...a hard hitting speaker who will give you a wakeup call that you'll never forget!"

Simon Hazeldine is in demand as a keynote speaker, consultant and facilitator in the areas of leadership, performance and persuasion.

His high impact speeches and seminars have received rave reviews and standing ovations across the globe.

Simon has run his high impact leadership, persuasion and performance seminars across five continents. His training programmes for sales managers and negotiators are currently being used in 28 countries around the world.

"Simon Hazeldine is a superb presenter who packs a punch!"

Simon is the bestselling author of four books:

The Inner Winner
Endorsed by success legend Brian Tracy

Bare Knuckle Selling
Foreword by sales and marketing legend Dr Joe Vitale

Bare Knuckle Negotiating
Foreword by multi-millionaire entrepreneur
Duncan Bannatyne from BBC TV's *Dragon's Den*

Bare Knuckle Customer Service
Foreword by multi-billionaire Michael Dell

DVD versions of *Bare Knuckle Selling*
and *Bare Knuckle Negotiating* are now available.

Simon has a Masters Degree in the Psychology of Performance and is a Certified Master Practitioner and Trainer of NLP.

He is a Fellow of the Institute of Sales & Marketing Management and a longstanding member of the Professional Speaking Association.

Prior to his current career, Simon provided event security and bodyguard services to celebrities from the television and music industry.

He has trained in the martial arts for over 20 years and also 'enjoys' running marathons (very slowly!).

To contact Simon about booking him to speak at your event please contact him at:

simon@simonhazeldine.com
www.simonhazeldine.com

Simon Hazeldine, E3, 1 Dexter Close, Quorn, Loughborough, Leicestershire LE12 8EH United Kingdom

"Simon Hazeldine has the experience, expertise and authority to make a big impact at your event."

E3
"Inspiring and Enabling Exceptional Performance"

Simon Hazeldine is the founder and Managing Director of specialist performance consultancy E3.

E3 provides a range of innovative consultancy and training solutions that will enable your organisation to perform at higher levels than ever before.

Our unique approach guarantees results.

We help a wide range of leading organisations with:

Sales Development
Helping Forward Thinking Sales Leaders Create High Performance Sales Forces that Deliver Exceptional Results

Negotiation
Helping You to Negotiate More Profitable Deals with Power and Confidence!

Influential and Impactful Communication
Helping You to Get Your Message Across With Clarity, Conviction and Confidence – Whatever the Audience Size or Situation!

Management & Leadership Development
Helping to Create World Class Managers and Leaders at Every Organisational Level

Organisational Development and Talent Management
Helping to Create High Performance Organisations That People Want To Belong To

www.E3ExceptionalPerformance.com

Lightning Source UK Ltd.
Milton Keynes UK
UKOW051221201212

203943UK00003B/21/P

9 781905 430628